Creating Research-Practice Partnerships in Education

Creating Research-Practice Partnerships in Education

William R. Penuel
Daniel J. Gallagher

HARVARD EDUCATION PRESS
CAMBRIDGE, MASSACHUSETTS

Paperback 978-1-68253-047-4
Library Edition 978-1-68253-048-1

Library of Congress Cataloging-in-Publication Data

Names: Penuel, William R., 1970- author. | Gallagher, Daniel J. (Writer on education), author.
Title: Creating research-practice partnerships in education / William R. Penuel, Daniel J. Gallagher.
Description: Cambridge, Massachusetts : Harvard Education Press, [2017] | Includes bibliographical references and index.
Identifiers: LCCN 2016056256| ISBN 9781682530474 (pbk.) | ISBN 9781682530481 (library edition)
Subjects: LCSH: Action research in education—United States. | Education and state—Research—United States. | Education—Research—United States. | Group work in education—United States.
Classification: LCC LB1028.24 .P46 2017 | DDC 370.72—dc23 LC record available at https://lccn.loc.gov/2016056256

Published by Harvard Education Press,
an imprint of the Harvard Education Publishing Group

Harvard Education Press
8 Story Street
Cambridge, MA 02138

Cover Design: Endpaper Studio
Cover Image: iStock.com/Carther

The typefaces used in this book are Minion Pro and Stone Sans.

Contents

Foreword

Who better to write a book about research-practice partnerships than two people—one a highly regarded education scholar and the other an accomplished educator and district administrator—who have been working together to build these mutualistic ventures? I have known and admired Bill Penuel for many years and have been encouraged and inspired by his commitment to partnership work. Dan Gallagher has made impressive contributions to the field through the work of his own partnership and his advocacy for partnerships in general. Of course, strong research-practice partnerships (RPPs) must go far beyond two key players, as this book makes very clear. Yet leaders like Bill and Dan can serve as models for readers involved with aspiring, developing, and extant RPPs in other places. I hope that this book—which draws on their expertise, as well as the experiences of a wide range of RPPs—will provide a valuable resource to encourage these leaders in their own work and will reach the broad audience it deserves.

Creating Research-Practice Partnerships in Education takes as its starting point Bill's seminal work with Cynthia Coburn, coauthor of chapter 2. They identify three defining characteristics of partnerships: careful, joint choice of the problem to work on; a commitment to ensuring that the work meets the needs of all involved; and the presence of intentional strategies to decide upon joint work. They also describe three major types of partnerships: research alliances, design-based research-practice partnerships, and networked improvement communities (while noting that there are many hybrid partnerships that exhibit various combinations of these types).

My experience with RPPs began through my long-time relationship with the University of Chicago's Consortium on Chicago School Research. There I learned of the value of conducting rigorous but useful and relevant research and I saw firsthand how Chicago Public Schools engaged with and acted upon our findings. In Chicago, I learned that partnerships are not only about getting more "research into practice." As this book makes abundantly clear, partnerships are also about bringing "practice into research." This is a two-way street with a reciprocal and recursive relationship between research and practice. Each is informed and improved by the other.

I brought my experiences from our Chicago partnership to the federal government, where the Institute of Education Sciences initiated an RPP grant program. At the Spencer Foundation, we also support RPPs. My colleagues Vivian Tseng and Lauren Supplee and I have written about partnerships, and in our writings we stress the importance of trusting relationships and good communication.[1] Trust enables partners to make it through the inevitable misunderstandings and miscommunications. That theme is prominent in this book as well, along with specific advice on how to build trust among diverse partners.

Because I had been most familiar with research alliances, I found this book especially helpful in expanding my horizons and teaching me about design-based partnerships and networked improvement communities. There are numerous examples of partnerships throughout the book so that all readers are sure to be able to identify with one or more. In addition to these many examples, the book contains many very specific suggestions, tools, and tips for developing and sustaining a partnership. There is also a nice emphasis on developing routines in partnerships that help partners navigate the many unexpected aspects of their work together. The word *agility* appears many times throughout this book, and *agile* is perhaps a good adjective for describing successful partners. As conditions change and partnerships evolve, it takes real agility on all parts to keep the work going and maturing.

The final chapter of this book discusses many important topics around the future of RPPs. What will it take to maintain this focus and develop it further? Who will fund the work? How do we build the infrastructure that's needed to make partnerships ubiquitous and commonplace, rather than unique and special? It is heartening to hear how some universities are changing not only to accommodate this kind of work, but also to encourage it. As education systems are further incentivized to become more analytic in their decision making, they too are more interested in partnering to help themselves improve. As both supply of and demand for partnerships increase, and as we learn more about what makes partnerships most effective, we can hope for a new generation of partnerships exhibiting even greater results.

That final chapter also contains a key insight about partnerships and about the improvement process. Many researchers and educators are still in search of the "magic bullet." What intervention, program, or tool can I create or adopt to solve big problems? This magic-bullet approach to improvement is sometimes exacerbated by calls for "evidence-based" policy making or practice improvement. These calls sometimes imply that a system can solve all its problems by faithfully implementing proven practices. My experience—along with the experiences of many others, including Bill and Dan—suggests that the approach to improvement described in this book is more likely to succeed. It takes many—researchers, educators, intermediaries, community members—working collaboratively and deliberately together to make significant, lasting improvements. Partnership work is characterized by careful analysis and constant iteration, improvement, and documentation. This book describes very well how partners can best work together and succeed in solving some of their most vexing problems. I hope that readers will take these ideas and suggestions to heart, try them out, and stick to it until they've achieved success.

John Q. Easton
Vice President, Programs
The Spencer Foundation

Preface

This book is intended to be a practical guide to help researchers and educational leaders in schools, districts, and community organizations form long-term collaborations with one another. The focus is on a particular kind of collaboration, *research-practice partnerships* (RPPs). RPPs are long-term collaborations between practitioners and researchers that are organized to investigate problems of practice and solutions for improving educational systems.

Now is an opportune time for a book on this topic for two reasons. First, there is an increased interest among policy makers, researchers, and educators today in the promise of research-practice partnerships. They see partnerships as ways to bring evidence to bear on educational decision making and as an approach to creating usable, effective innovations. Thus, the hunger for evidence and for strategies to overcome challenges of partnerships is higher than ever in recent educational history. Second, there is now both a growing body of scholarship on and direct experience of partnerships from which we can draw to support claims about how best to organize partnerships effectively.

This book is grounded in both scholarship and the wisdom of practice. We rely on narratives as a tool to bring to life the dynamics of partnership, especially narratives that draw on our own experiences as leaders of RPPs. Each of us brings a long history of involvement with partnerships, but from the different positions of researcher (Bill) and educator (Dan). At the same time, the reason we have written this book together is that we share certain perspectives on the value of partnerships and enjoy working together. We also see partnerships as a way for us to be engaged in work that the other person does that we love to have a part in: for Bill, that's leading professional development and building teachers' capacity to work together for change, and for Dan, it's being part of educational research on curricular innovations and scaling educational change efforts. Also, for the past three years, we have co-led workshops for researchers and educators about partnerships, helping them learn more about the nature of partnership work and develop the skills and dispositions we think are necessary for this kind of work.

Bill started out his career in educational research working in the central office at Metropolitan Nashville Public Schools in the mid-1990s. His entry into education research coincided with early efforts by scientists learning to scale up innovations in math, science, and writing in the school district. It was an exciting effort, but a school board controversy led to the demise of these efforts, which were led locally by Vanderbilt researchers John Bransford, Susan Goldman, and Jim Pellegrino. For Bill, the experience was formative in that it underscored how valuable it could be for researchers to engage collaboratively at the district level to expand access to powerful learning innovations to all children, as well as just how vulnerable such efforts could be to political pressures and dynamics.

Since that time, Bill has spent his career in a nonprofit research organization (SRI International) and in a university (University of Colorado Boulder). His research has expanded beyond evaluation to the design and implementation of innovations in science, mathematics, and literacy for children in preschools, middle schools, high schools, and afterschool programs for youth of all ages. Since 2007, he has partnered with the Denver Public Schools, supporting their math and science teams. The examples in the book draw extensively from this partnership, as well as earlier efforts involving design work with school districts and groups of teachers looking to have systemwide impacts on teaching and learning in mathematics and science education.

For his part, Dan started out in research, and landed eventually in a leadership position in a major urban school district, the Seattle Public Schools. He began as a lab scientist in molecular biology and physiology in Colorado and Seattle, but his desire to serve and have a bigger impact on the world led him to pursue a teaching career. He taught high school science in the Bellevue Public Schools in Washington, and he eventually became an instructional coach and curriculum developer in that school district. In those roles at Bellevue, he sought education research to inform his work with teachers and began to reach out to researchers like Charles W. (Andy) Anderson of Michigan State University, who was developing curriculum and assessments and also looking for places to test out his materials. Dan's continued engagement with researchers and gracious, informal mentors like Anderson and Philip Bell of the University of Washington honed his ability to form and sustain RPPs. Ultimately, Dan became a co–principal investigator on multiple large scale-up grants with Anderson funded by the National Science Foundation. He has also initiated and led two Math-Science Partnership grants from the state of Washington as the principal investigator. By choosing to position himself with fellow practitioners in school districts and partner with researchers in universities, Dan aims to bring the two communities together to improve experiences for students. Recently, to further deepen his knowledge and skills as a systems-level educational leader, he began to pursue an EdD at the University of Washington. These experiences give him a unique perspective on living inside multiple RPPs from the district role. Dan is now Director of Career and College Readiness in Seattle Public Schools.

From these brief descriptions, we hope readers will get a better sense of where we are coming from and why we are passionate about partnerships. At the same time, we know that the vast majority of our experience in partnerships locates us in one corner of the partnership world, namely partnerships between district central offices and university researchers working in the areas of mathematics and science. We have sought to describe the activities of partnerships focused on other issues and composed of different types of organizations—for instance, those involving research nonprofits and community organizations—by drawing on others' experiences.

We also recognize that our perspectives come from relatively privileged places within our institutions and within the broader society. We are leaders within large organizations, and our work has been well resourced by the external funding we've received. We are also two white men in a society that affords us a certain power to act that people of other racial backgrounds and gender identities might not have. Throughout the book, we have brought in other voices from partnerships led by people from nondominant backgrounds to expand the perspectives we give from our own experience. Still, we know that our own position within society limits what we can say with confidence here. We hope ours is one among many books on partnerships in the coming years, and that there will be more scholarship in this area by scholars of color to expand what it means to be in partnership.

For both of us, the content of the book reflects the core of our work as individuals in our respective organizations. For Bill, it represents a synthesis of ideas about how to work in partnership as a researcher developed across two decades of joint projects with school districts and community organizations. For Dan, writing about partnership is a way to help him clarify and articulate the strategies he's developed over the years for working productively with researchers. Individually and together, we're always grateful that people seem interested enough to stick around and engage with us on the topic of partnerships. We hope that readers will find in this book something that is both interesting and practical, something that rings true even if the experiences we describe are unfamiliar. Most of all, we hope it inspires you to go out and start a research-practice partnership.

1

Why Research-Practice Partnerships?

"We need more researchers on speed dial," announced Jim Ryan, a curriculum director from San Francisco Unified School District. Jim had come to a meeting we held in Boulder, Colorado, in the summer of 2014, to bring together leaders of eleven different research-practice partnerships (RPPs) from across the United States. Jim already had on speed dial his research partners from the Strategic Education Research Partnership, and he greatly valued their contributions to his district's improvement efforts. He often consulted with them on district policies and programs. To Jim, the value of his partners was in his ongoing relationship with them, the fact that they helped him to tackle some of the most pressing problems he faced.

Many researchers are likewise interested in doing work that is more relevant and useful to people like Jim. In fact, those at the Boulder meeting that summer were united by a commitment to explore new ways of relating research and practice—to work, over the long term, to research pressing problems of practice and to test solutions to address them. None of us had an easy answer for Jim about how to get more researchers on speed dial for education leaders like him. We were all trying to figure out how to prepare both researchers and education leaders for working in research-practice partnerships.

This book, a response to Jim's call and to the need for resources for partnerships, provides background and guidance on building and sustaining RPPs. In our years as active leaders in RPPs, we have seen again and again the need for practical guidance, for both researchers and educators, on the knowledge and skills they must have to work together on problems of practice over the long haul. Developing the right knowledge and skills is only half the challenge, though. Education leaders and researchers need to approach one another with a listening ear, ready to learn from one another and with respect for what the other brings to the partnership. The educator-researcher partnership is a process in which those involved learn together how to address problems of practice through their joint work. Neither partner knows ahead of time precisely which efforts will be successful, under what conditions, or for whom.

The need to share practical solutions to the challenges of building and sustaining partnerships is becoming more urgent. Fueled by new sources of funding and a belief in the promise of RPPs for designing and testing interventions, many people are forming new collaborations. In this book, we describe strategies that have worked in our own partnerships and in others for building a solid foundation for partnerships, designing and testing solutions to problems of practice, and responding to the predictable bumps in the road that partnerships encounter. Although no partnership's situation is the same as any other, our own experience of sharing stories about partnership successes and challenges gives us hope that others can learn from case studies of the kind we present here. In addition, we know that practical tools and templates of the kind we provide at the end of the book are essential resources for building and sustaining a healthy partnership.

THE DIVIDE BETWEEN HOW EDUCATION RESEARCH IS PRODUCED AND USED TODAY

Great research is happening all the time—the kind of research that generates the strong evidence that policies call for to inform practice. But much of this research takes place on one side of a big divide, largely ignoring the problems that persist in the education system on the other. In this section we describe this divide, before discussing how partnerships can help bridge it in the next section.

For more than a decade, the field of education research has been developing strong evidence on a whole host of topics. The US Department of Education's What Works Clearinghouse (WWC) summarizes the results of studies that examine the impact of various programs and policies. The Department of Education has reviewed over eleven thousand studies for the WWC and written practice guides, intervention reports, and single-study reviews to summarize some of the best evidence of what works in education.[1] The WWC can be a tremendous resource for people like Jim Ryan and other curriculum leaders across the United States who oversee a wide variety of programs in math and science education. Lots of leaders *do* consult the WWC, but it's only one resource they use to inform their decisions and includes only some of what they need from research to guide their work.

About one in five education leaders turns to the WWC on a regular basis. But it is not the most popular place leaders turn to for research. In a recent study conducted as part of the National Center for Research in Policy and Practice, Bill and colleagues surveyed more than seven hundred school and district leaders about where they accessed research and how they used it.[2] They found that leaders turned most often to their peers and their professional associations for research. The survey results also showed that the kind of research school and district leaders find useful is not the kind of research available in the WWC. Most reported finding useful studies that provide them with tools or frameworks for thinking about their district's problems in a different way. Only a few said they find useful the kinds of impact studies that generate evidence of what works.

Another factor limiting the value of the kinds of impact studies reviewed in the WWC is the nature of education leaders' work. They often need to make decisions about policies and programs that don't yet have evidence to support them. Research almost always lags behind policy making, leaving leaders without the evidence they need when they need it.[3] Further, leaders do not only select new policies and programs; their jobs entail diverse other tasks, like monitoring program implementation and designing professional development. For those tasks, they find other kinds of resources more useful, such as frameworks from research they can use to help them design programs.[4] Researchers, meanwhile, work in a system that does not reward them for tackling problems of how to apply such frameworks to practical challenges faced by education leaders. Instead, it gives them the biggest rewards for coming up with new frameworks and theories to supplant their own and colleagues' old ones.

When educators and researchers do manage to work productively together, the results can be strong, but educators can be left trying to figure out how to sustain evidence-based programs after the researchers' funding for a project ends. To see the limitations of the current system, we turn to a story that on the surface is a success story from the past decade—one that generated strong evidence of the effectiveness of a middle-school math program in a wide variety of contexts. In our view, though, this story is also a cautionary tale that highlights the problems we are seeking to change.

What Happened When the Research Ended? The Story of SimCalc MathWorlds

Several years ago, Bill and his colleague Barry Fishman set out to answer what they thought was a straightforward question: What happens to an effective intervention when the research ends? Our colleagues at SRI International and the University of Massachusetts had just finished an experimental study in Texas of a middle-school mathematics program called SimCalc MathWorlds. The study had been extraordinarily successful, showing gains in student achievement among both Latino and white students, and among both lower-income and higher-income students.[5] Given these results, Bill and Barry assumed that most teachers would still be using the program a year later.

In fact, just over half of the teachers were still using the program with their students. Those teachers had students who were more economically advantaged and higher achieving than the teachers no longer using the program. It was a classic case of what sociologist Robert Merton called the "Matthew Effect," so named for the passage in the Book of Matthew (25:29), "Whoever has will be given more, and they will have an abundance. Whoever does not have, even what they have will be taken from them."[6] Bill and Barry were not the first to document Matthew Effects in education, but they were surprised to see them here, after such a successful study that had proven the program's promise for students from a wide variety of backgrounds.[7]

A closer look at the data shed light on their findings. Teachers who perceived that SimCalc MathWorlds aligned with their own or their school's goals for reform were more likely to still be using the program. This suggested the importance of the local context to teachers. Once the research ended, teachers were no longer beholden to researchers' demands on their time and their participation was no longer paid, so local goals returned to the foreground. Teachers who viewed local goals as aligned with the use of SimCalc continued to use the program, while teachers who did not see a connection were much more likely to stop using it.

What's the Matter with Our Research and Development Infrastructure?

When the SimCalc study ended, researchers discontinued support for implementing the program. They didn't have any more funds to incentivize teacher participation with stipends. They internalized different messages about whether SimCalc supported their school or district's local goals, and those that thought the materials didn't support local goals were more likely to stop using it. Teachers are bombarded with information about what they should be doing in class with their students; on their own, it's difficult for them to make sense of how a program like SimCalc, introduced by a research team that's no longer around to help, fits in with the multiple and changing messages they get about what and how to teach.

And because the schools involved in the study were spread across the state, there was no single district office to appeal to for ongoing support. If a district leader was excited by the results, he or she may not have been able to convince a supervisor to invest in one program of the myriad other interventions and opportunities the district was pursuing. A new research study that brings new funding may be more attractive than trying to sustain a proven program without dedicated resources.

It was no one's responsibility to figure out how to sustain SimCalc MathWorlds after the research ended in the settings where it was implemented. No one had the job of convincing teachers of low-income and Latino students to continue to use it, either. There wasn't the possibility of extending the grant to study the program another year—the grant was over. And any effort to sustain the program was up against the barriers we've described of keeping it aligned with changing district environments.

Many researchers find this kind of situation frustrating. Some researchers wonder why school and district leaders ignore compelling evidence of what works. Other researchers understand the need for ongoing support for programs but can't find the time to help a district sort out how to sustain a program once the research ends, because they must turn to new work for which they have funding. Both groups of researchers can be haunted by a sense of futility—a feeling that research cannot have much of an impact on local policy and practice. And thus the system leaves educators everywhere with few, if any, researchers on speed dial they can call for help to address their most pressing problems of practice.

The SimCalc MathWorlds story is unusual only in one respect: the program worked and proved effective in a wide variety of contexts. As in other fields, many interventions in education do not work; that is, they do not have a big impact on teaching and learning. But even when something works, there may not be resources available to continue implementing it. Every time an intervention is brought to scale through an externally funded research study, funds for continued implementation support dry up when the study ends.

Many people think the issue has a simple fix: if a program works, then schools and districts should continue to use it. After all, they have strong incentives and pressures from accountability systems to find programs that can increase student test scores. This view ignores the complexities of implementation, however. Implementing a program like SimCalc requires materials, ongoing professional development, and support for teachers and principals to integrate the program into their classrooms and schools. After the research ends, though, there's no obvious source of funding for these things.

RESEARCH-PRACTICE PARTNERSHIPS: A DIFFERENT WAY OF WORKING TOGETHER

The SimCalc team would not give up its hope of spreading and sustaining SimCalc MathWorlds. It took a new setting—a large school district in Florida—and a completely different approach to working with educators to accomplish their aim. They formed a *research-practice partnership*—a long-term collaboration between the school district and the research team, organized around the district's own problems of practice.[8] This alternate approach involves researchers and educators working together to study educational problems and solutions to those problems. Most importantly, researchers stick around to investigate conditions under which an effective innovation can be sustained equitably.

The partners in this new endeavor were researchers from SRI International, district leaders and mathematics teachers from Pinellas County School District, and faculty at the University of South Florida St. Petersburg, a local institution that already had a long-term arrangement with the district to provide teacher professional development. They began by focusing on a problem the district wanted to solve, namely low achievement in middle-school mathematics. Researchers and practitioners worked together to identify some core ideas that they judged to be mathematically important and also difficult to teach and learn. They looked together at the just-adopted Next Generation Sunshine State Standards (Florida's version of the Common Core State Standards) to see how the standards overlapped with their ideas and with available SimCalc MathWorlds curriculum materials. On the basis of their analysis, they selected a seventh-grade unit on rate and proportionality.

The team didn't just reimplement the unit as it had been written for Texas students. They made both small and large changes to the unit to better fit the local context. Small changes included replacing Texan place names with Floridian ones. Larger changes included changing some mathematics terminology and graphs that students had to use or interpret, to be consistent with Florida content standards. By making these changes, the team hoped to create materials that teachers would readily recognize as fitting with their local school and district demands for what they were supposed to teach.

The team worked collaboratively with a small group of researchers, district leaders, and teachers to make these adaptations. This was a shift from how they had worked in Texas, when development was led by professional curriculum writers working relatively independently to write lessons. By creating a cadre of teacher-leaders, they hoped to build ownership among them that would translate into local teacher advocacy when it came time to scale the unit throughout the district.

The SimCalc partnership created professional development designs that could be used by others, developed a teacher edition of the student materials, and supplied the technology needed to implement the materials. Together, these elements formed what the researchers called an integrated *curricular activity system*—that is, a set of activities and resources that fit together and could serve as a kind of "portable infrastructure" for supporting implementation in a variety of schools within the district.[9] SRI laid this groundwork by passing responsibility for professional development to faculty members at the University of South Florida St. Petersburg after the first year. The university was a logical partner for ensuring the sustainability of the project since it was already the primary professional development provider to the school district. Further, the university was motivated to participate since the program aligned with its own goal of enhancing its capacity to prepare teachers to integrate technology effectively into their instruction.

In an initial testing phase, the partnership focused on a small number of teachers and schools in order to establish evidence that SimCalc could work in Pinellas County prior to scaling it there. Unlike in the prior Texas study, in Florida researchers offered no special incentives for teachers who agreed to implement the units. They were concerned that incentives would create "hothouse" conditions that could not replicate what might happen in the everyday environment in the school district, where teachers are expected to implement a new unit without any financial incentive to do so. But the researchers, mindful of the risk of asking too much of the teachers, sought to minimize the burden on them by reducing the amount of data they collected from them.

Remarkably—or perhaps not remarkably at all, given the thoughtfulness with which the partnership designed and supported implementation—the team replicated the strong student learning gains they had observed in their randomized controlled trial. Though they did not conduct another experiment, they compared the gains to that of the treatment group and to the original comparison group, and found that the gains and advantage of the SimCalc group relative to the original comparison group were the same. (See Tools and Templates, exhibit 1: "Communicating the Importance of Partnerships for Addressing Implementation.")

Key Characteristics of Research-Practice Partnerships

The SimCalc partnership illustrates several key features of RPPs.

A focus on problems of practice. First, the partnership is focused on *problems of practice* faced by the school district. This focus makes partnership research different from typical, researcher-initiated studies. Such studies are primarily intended to advance knowledge and theory, and whether a proposed study constitutes an advance is judged by other researchers, not by education leaders or teachers. The focus is also different from policy evaluations that examine the impact of federal and state policies, which may or may not have buy-in from local educators. In this case, the focal problem of practice was determined jointly by the partners and not decided ahead of time by either researchers or educators. It was a problem that different groups of stakeholders cared about solving.

Long-term commitment. RPPs are *long term*; that is, the partners have an open-ended commitment to working with one another over time. The long-term nature of these partnerships allows researchers and educators to take up problems of implementation and sustainability together, long after researchers would normally have left the scene. It also means that they often require multiple sources and cycles of funding to sustain. Over time, as both funders' demands and focal problems change, so do partnerships' activities. A long-term partnership is one that therefore likely has multiple lines of work that the researchers and educators have pursued together.

A mutualistic relationship. Another feature of RPPs is that they are *mutualistic*; both parties are working toward a shared goal in ways that respect the priorities of each. In seeking to address problems of practice, some researchers go so far as to help collaboratively design and test solutions to problems that districts face, while others research possible solutions and study the solutions districts choose or design. Either way, partnerships attend to the distinct needs of individual partners. A good partnership can amplify the voices and strengthen the initiatives of a district leader, and it can help a researcher execute a research design that is necessary to obtain future funding or help secure publication in a journal. It can also give voice to teachers, parents, community members, and students, when representatives from these groups are included in activities to define problems and design solutions. Mutualism entails attending to the partners' shared *and* individually held goals.

Partnerships don't leave mutualism to chance: they employ *intentional strategies* to make sure each partner's needs are met and goals are attended to. Such a strategy can be as simple as a memorandum of understanding, or it can take the more elaborate form of a governing board that helps shape a long-term research agenda. Still other partnerships have explicit agreements about how specific research questions will be addressed and even when and with whom results can be shared.[10] The process of developing a new proposal to a funding agency is also an occasion for making sure not only that partners agree on key goals but also that each partner understands what resources are necessary to accomplish specific activities designed to meet those goals. As we discuss later in this book, there are a variety of everyday strategies for ensuring mutualism that are critical to building and maintaining a partnership.

Generation of original analyses. Another important characteristic of RPPs is that they produce *original analyses* that go beyond tabulations of administrative data readily available to schools. Schools and districts are awash in data on student achievement, and many also have databases they can query to ask specific questions about the performance of particular schools or subgroups of students. RPPs go beyond repackaging existing data. Many partnerships build data archives that draw from several different sources, including outside the education system. Some, like the Consortium on Chicago School Research (CCSR), have for decades collected data directly from teachers, parents, and students. In CCSR's case, these were not data that the district had collected before, and the district on its own might not have had the inclination or capacity to collect and analyze these data. Analyses of these data led to new insights about the organizational supports needed to improve schools, like high levels of trust among teachers in a school. The partnership expressed its findings as a framework and published a book, one that has already proven useful for education leaders across the country.[11]

The Promise of Research-Practice Partnerships for Developing Evidence-Based Programs

The case of SimCalc shows how a partnership can help a district to adapt a program that has been tested and proven effective elsewhere. But can a partnership *develop* a program and then *test* it using rigorous research? In other words, can a partnership create an "evidence-based program" whole cloth? Although our current research and development infrastructure puts researchers in the driver's seat for developing programs, there is strong evidence that partnerships can also develop effective programs.

A good example comes from the Strategic Education Research Partnership (SERP), Jim Ryan's partners mentioned at the beginning of this chapter. In addition to its partnerships with San Francisco Unified and Boston Public Schools, SERP has convened a network comprising multiple districts called the Minority Student Achievement Network, or MSAN. MSAN's main focus is on educational equity for students from nondominant communities. A persistent problem for many districts is the high rate at which students fail algebra. The failure rates are higher among districts that have mandated early algebra (i.e., students must take algebra in the eighth grade). The problem is urgent since algebra has been identified as a "gatekeeper" course for access to higher education, meaning those who do not pass it are less likely to enter college.[12] To address this problem, researchers worked with leaders in MSAN districts to collaboratively design "AlgebraByExample," an intervention that would target students of color but take place in regular classrooms so as not to isolate students in pullout programs.

The project drew on a key finding in the learning sciences, namely that students learn best from "interleaved worked examples." A worked example comprises a set of instructions for how to solve a particular type of problem, along with an example problem that shows the step-by-step solution. Interleaving refers to putting worked examples in between problem sets that students are asked to solve independently. There is strong evidence that interleaved worked examples enhance student learning.[13]

Though the finding about worked examples is a robust one, translating basic research into a usable intervention is a complex process. The MSAN partnership undertook this task by conducting cycles of design research—a type of research in which interventions are tested and iteratively refined in a few classrooms. Over several years, they developed the forty-two assignments that made up AlgebraByExample intervention. Teacher co-designers played a critical role in designing these assignments, reviewing, revising, and reshaping them to better meet the needs of their students.

Researchers carried out a series of studies that culminated in a random assignment study. Twenty-five teachers were randomly assigned to implement AlgebraByExample assignments or to implement their district curriculum. They found a strong positive effect of the intervention and published the results in a peer-reviewed journal.[14] Both the school district's goals for improving student performance and the researchers' goals for advancing theory and knowledge in their field were met through this partnership between research and practice.

The AlgebraByExample story is not an isolated instance of a research-practice partnership developing *and* testing an effective intervention. A recent review found a number of other interventions designed by partnerships in recent years that demonstrated a positive impact on student learning as reported in peer-reviewed journal articles.[15] These include targeted interventions like AlgebraByExample, full curriculum units, and formative assessment interventions. No doubt, this review missed many other interventions whose origins in partnerships were simply not documented in peer-reviewed publications. Despite the clear success of partnerships in developing and testing interventions, however, the jury is still out on the relative effectiveness and efficiency of partnerships for developing evidence-based programs. It leads to a natural question, too: If partnerships can produce successful interventions, why aren't they more common?

The Challenges of Research-Practice Partnerships

Beyond the challenges of obtaining resources necessary for partnerships—challenges linked to how research is funded—there are a number of difficulties that partnerships face in getting off the ground. It's hard to know where to begin a partnership. The work of school districts is multifaceted and complex. To a researcher looking from the outside in, it's hard to see where the most impact can be realized. For an education leader looking out, it's hard to sift through the multiple requests from researchers asking to collaborate. Nearly every researcher says that they want to "partner" with a district, but often this means little more than them wanting access to data or sites where researchers can test their interventions. And even those who are genuinely interested in a partnership can't possibly understand *a priori* how to be a good partner to an unfamiliar district.

We have written elsewhere about the wobbly start of a partnership between Bellevue Public Schools and the University of Washington.[16] That partnership, in which Dan was a key player for the district and in which Bill was a researcher, merits consideration here as a microcosm of partnership challenges—and the rewards of overcoming them.

The Bellevue-UW partnership was initiated when the Bellevue superintendent reached out to UW faculty member John Bransford. The superintendent asked John's team to perform a "curriculum audit" focused on how well the district's curriculum reflected the principles of the recently published National Research Council volume, *How People Learn*, for which Bransford served as a lead author.[17] Around that time, the superintendent had introduced a web platform where teachers could access the district's adopted curriculum materials, and was eager to increase teachers' use of it. Once the UW researchers got started, however, they saw a different opportunity for engaging with the district that went beyond the curriculum audit. Meanwhile, a dispute arose between the teachers' association and the district about the online platform, and the superintendent who had first reached out passed away suddenly. Over the next few years, the team found its way into a productive line of work focused on augmenting the kit-based science curriculum that the district had adopted at the elementary level. But the journey was not without false starts and worry about the fate of this emerging partnership.

For one, developing a stable focus for the work of the partnership proved difficult. Each side saw a different opportunity in working together, and perceived different strengths and needs in the other. The partners didn't know much about each other at the beginning, either as individuals or as institutions with particular histories. And the partnership faced turnover and political turbulence, even before it got off the ground.

Though this particular partnership survived this initial trial, many more do not, and for good reason. Sometimes researchers don't bring the right disposition to the work. They think they understand the district's problems, even before they get to know them. Or they view the politics that are at the core of all district activities as a nuisance, rather than something to engage directly as a necessary part of partnership work. For their part, district leaders may misjudge the particular strengths and weaknesses of researchers they seek out. They may not communicate well or easily how the system functions to empower researchers as joint problem solvers. The trust may not exist to do so, either within the district or between the sets of partners.

Even when partnerships get off the ground, maintaining them is not easy. There are no major sources of funding for partnerships to operate over the long haul. Few funders at present provide money for the basic infrastructure of partnerships—for example, a facilitator for the partnership just to ensure the smooth coordination of work, or a data archive that can serve as a resource for analysis. In partnership work, there are no guarantees of long-term stability, only contingencies and the commitments of fallible, well-meaning people to work together.

The risks are not the same for researchers and educators in partnership, either. University incentive systems for researchers will look askance at efforts, especially from junior scholars, to conduct work in partnership with practitioners.[18] Junior faculty members are routinely cautioned, "Wait until you get tenure to do this kind of work. It's messy, and it might not pan out." Many tenure committees view partnership work primarily as a form of service, rather than as research, which is more highly valued. As a result, many junior researchers do not initiate partnerships. Later, when they have reached a point in their careers when they can afford the risk, they may have developed dispositions and approaches to research that are not conducive to partnership work.

While there are risks on both sides of a partnership, the risks are unquestionably greater for educators. Their jobs are on the line in a more direct way than researchers' are, since they are more accountable to the *success* of the partnership. A researcher can write about an unsuccessful initiative as an "interesting failure," but an educator can take little comfort in failure. Educators may also be called to defend partnerships that others may view as a distraction from district priorities.

WHY WE THINK IT IS WORTH INVESTING IN RESEARCH-PRACTICE PARTNERSHIPS

Despite the many challenges of RPPs, we think that for some partners and initiatives, the investment is worth it. We fall on the side of partnerships, because we believe the traditional approach leaves educators in a difficult spot when trying to solve challenging problems of sustainability without resources to do so, as the original SimCalc study did. The researcher-driven approach, moreover, produces many innovations that don't fit into the existing infrastructures of schools and districts. By contrast, the long-term nature of partnerships provides opportunities for researchers and educators to work together to figure out how to make innovations work across a range of settings. In addition, the focus on developing solutions to problems of practice makes the questions researchers pursue and the solutions that are developed more relevant and useful to practice.

For us, working in partnership is some of the most meaningful time we spend in our jobs. In partnerships, we feel like we can make a difference, even when we struggle to succeed. We also learn a great deal in partnerships—not only about each other as researchers and educators, but also about what it takes to support meaningful improvements to teaching and learning at the scale of a district or beyond. At the same time, we do not think that all partnerships are good bets for those involved. We'll discuss when to end a partnership later in this book, and throughout, we'll provide tips for helping manage the ups and downs of partnerships that are just part of the work. In the coming chapters, we'll discuss how to approach the early stages of partnership development, how to structure initial projects, how to promote and maintain mutualism, how to sustain partnerships, and how to organize research projects over time.

But we are also hopeful about partnerships, and that is why we are writing this book. Many of the partnerships we describe have survived many challenges and are alive and well today. We've seen truly successful partnerships in our own work, and we've used a combination of our direct experience and systematic inquiry to identify the tools and practices that make partnerships successful. This book presents our best synthesis of what we've learned so far.

2

Varieties of Working Relationships Between Educators and Researchers

with Cynthia E. Coburn

Researchers and practitioners can work together in many productive ways; most of these are not research-practice partnerships. Some are *vendor-client* relationships, such as when districts hire researchers to provide a professional development series or conduct an evaluation. Sometimes, a district is just a site for data collection; that is, it's a place where researchers can find teachers and students to participate in research they've defined ahead of time. Both arrangements require collaboration, but in these cases, the goals are defined primarily by one partner, and there is no open-ended commitment to working with one another. In a partnership, the partners jointly decide on the focus of their work and jointly define the issues involved. They also have some common values that shape the kinds of solutions they develop together.

Cynthia E. Coburn is a professor at the School of Education and Social Policy at Northwestern University. She studies the relationship between instructional policy and teachers' classroom practices in urban schools.

Even among RPPs, there is variety in how educators and researchers work together. In some partnerships, researchers are evaluators. By retaining independence and objectivity, evaluators can help districts provide unbiased evidence to policy makers and other stakeholders. In other partnerships, researchers collaborate more actively to co-design solutions to specific problems of practice. In such partnerships, researchers may also commit to supporting implementation of those solutions and to troubleshooting the inevitable challenges associated with implementation. In partnerships that take on multiple lines of work, researchers and educators may work together differently in each.

In this chapter, we contrast some common relationships between researchers and educators within RPPs as a way to help answer the question, "Is my relationship a research-practice partnership?" We then describe three different types of partnerships that illustrate some of the most common ways that RPPs are organized. We present this typology of partnerships as a model for prospective partners to examine and adapt when organizing their own partnerships. This typology was developed by two of us (Cynthia and Bill) and a colleague, Kimberly Geil, as part of a project conducted for the William T. Grant Foundation.

TWO TYPES OF RELATIONSHIPS THAT ARE NOT PARTNERSHIPS

Before we define what a partnership is, it's important to distinguish what we mean by "partnership" from how the term is often used. The word *partnership* is used to describe many different kinds of relationships between researchers and educators. In addition, there are many relationships between researchers and educators that are long-term, involve researchers conducting original analyses, and focus on problems of practice—three key characteristics of partnerships we named in chapter 1—but still do not meet our definition of partnership.

The two types of relationships we describe next—leaders hiring researchers as experts or vendors, and researchers seeking schools and districts as sites for studies—are sometimes called "partnerships," but they do not meet two of our key criteria for a research-practice partnership. First, one side decides on the focus of the work, and thus the relationship is not mutualistic as we define that term for partnerships. Second, the relationships are intentionally organized, but not in a way to foster mutualism. One side sets the terms for the relationship and has authority to decide on the focus of work and judge whether the terms of any agreements have been met. There are formal contracts and agreements, but it is fair to say that one side is in the dominant negotiating position when these are developed.

The types of relationships we describe next are especially appropriate when the goals, activities, and expected roles of either the researchers or educators are clear and specified ahead of time. In other words, to be productive and valuable, a relationship between researchers and educators does not need to be an RPP.

Leaders Hiring Researchers as Experts and Vendors

Education leaders sometimes engage researchers to support specific aims of schools and districts, including in advisory or training capacities. The researcher is hired by or volunteers services for the education leaders, who define the terms of the engagement. Because in these cases the leaders decide on the goals and terms of the relationship, we do not consider them to be RPPs.

For example, a district curriculum leader might call a researcher she knows is knowledgeable about curriculum writing with teachers to ask for advice on writing an English language arts curriculum aligned to new standards. Or an associate superintendent might invite a researcher with expertise in leadership to present their framework for leadership. In these cases, the researcher might be paid a consulting fee, or might offer advice or give a talk without expectation of payment. In both instances, district leaders ask researchers to serve their aims, without consideration for goals the researchers might adopt if they were in the leaders' situation.

More extended engagements may involve one or more formal contracts under which researchers perform services for an educational organization, such as professional development for leaders or teachers. A state leader might reach out to experts in social and emotional learning to ask that they provide a one-year professional development program on strategies for teachers to foster greater empathy among their students. The researchers might have input regarding the details of the program, but again the educational organization's aims and constraints largely define the engagement. A researcher may also be contracted to provide evaluation services. For example, a district evaluation specialist might reach out to a researcher specializing in teacher evaluation systems to study a new district initiative. The researcher may negotiate the cost and scope of the evaluation, but the district defines the evaluation questions, the program, and even some of the outcome measures.

Occasionally, districts hire researchers to help build the organizational capacity for improving the performance of a given district function. The Strategic Data Fellowship program at the Center for Education Policy Research at Harvard University is one such arrangement. It is a two-year program that develops data strategists in districts where they can influence policy decisions that affect student outcomes. Fellows recruited into the program receive professional development in measurement and analysis, leadership and change management, and education policy. Districts pay for the salaries of Strategic Data Fellows—who may be current employees of the district or people from outside the district. Capacity-building engagements like the Strategic Data Fellowship program are similar to many RPPs that aim specifically to increase the capacity of educational systems for improving teaching and learning outcomes. However, they are not RPPs as we define them here, because the joint endeavor has no aim to produce new knowledge about capacity building. The program draws on research but does not produce original research about its activities.

Researchers Seeking Schools and Districts as Sites for Studies

Just as education leaders approach researchers with an already-formed need and approach, researchers also approach districts with specific ideas for studies. They tell the teachers, principals, and districts what they plan to do, what will be expected of participants, and how (if at all) participants will be compensated. The researchers may say they are looking for a "partner" when they approach educators to be part of a grant-funded study, but the researcher has already defined the problem to address, the research questions, and the strategy for answering those questions. In this situation, schools and districts are mainly sites for research projects.

To say that a school or district is a site and not a partner in this typical scenario is not to question the researchers' motives. In all fairness, many likely care a great deal about improving educational outcomes for students.

They bring their own particular theoretical perspective on the problems schools and districts face, which can sometimes expand how district leaders view these problems. District leaders may grant such research requests in hopes the fresh perspective will be valuable. Moreover, the research findings might be very useful to the school district, especially if researchers happen to be focused on an area that is of particular interest to district leaders.

While it is far from ideal that researchers often define studies with little or no input from leaders, this approach is typical because of how funding works. Education leaders' views are excluded from three key stages in the funding process. First, researchers may have opportunities to provide input that shapes funders' solicitations or requests for proposals. Most funding for research in education comes from federal agencies, like the US Department of Education and the National Science Foundation, and from private foundations. Second, the solicitations typically are for "researcher-initiated" grants, proposals in which researchers pitch ideas aligned to the funder's priorities. Grant programs that call for partnerships (such as the Institute of Education Sciences' Researcher-Practitioner Partnerships in Education Research program) are the exception. Finally, the peer reviewers who evaluate are also typically researchers.

RESEARCH-PRACTICE PARTNERSHIPS

In the types of relationships we've just described, either educators' or researchers' goals drive the arrangement, but in partnerships both partners' aims are met. In addition, the agreements put in place establish formal processes for ensuring that the focus of work is jointly negotiated. Our experience tells us there are three telltale signs that a relationship is a partnership.

The first indicator is that the problem of practice that educators and researchers say they are working on is one that they've arrived at through some deliberation and negotiation. Partners should be able to describe how their own initial understanding of the problem has shifted over time as a consequence of working jointly toward a common understanding of the issue. Long-term partnerships also likely have stories about how, as partners' priorities have changed over time, they have renegotiated the focus of their joint work and the problems they set out to solve. In our experience, while partners can tell such stories, they aren't always the same from partner to partner: there's never a single story of a partnership, even in successful long-term ones.

When we speak to research audiences, we often invite researchers who are thinking about partnerships to look at the slide decks they present to colleagues at conferences and other professional gatherings. We ask them to perform what we call the "Slide Two Test." Slide two is typically where researchers present the "problem" they are addressing. We ask researchers to consider what would happen if they showed their second slide to educators in the districts where they conduct their work. Would educators see themselves in the problem statement and say, "Yes, that's what we're working on together"? If the answer is yes, then the focal problems have most likely been jointly negotiated and don't represent only the researcher's perspective.

We could ask the same thing of educators in partnerships, but we'd need to look for a different set of indicators that their way of framing the problem reflects the influence of their research partner. We might look for evidence of uptake of "big ideas" in educators' statements of the problem they are working on in the partnership. We—Bill and Cynthia, with colleagues from Northwestern University and the University of Colorado Boulder—did that for a pair of RPPs we studied, and we found strong evidence of uptake of some of those ideas across a wide variety of district partners. These were in partnerships where we knew there was lots of discussion between researchers and educators about the problems they were focusing on together.

A second sign that a relationship is a partnership is that the partnership's shared aims and activities also meet the distinctive needs of each partner. For educators, that might manifest as a concern for making sure that the research is conducted in a manner that will permit the research partner to publish results in a peer-reviewed journal. For researchers, a concern for the educators' goals might be manifest in the ways that they allow their research questions to be shaped by the partner organization's priorities for improvement. In a partnership, the partners understand their shared aims, their individual aims, and how each partner has accommodated the other to engage in joint work together.

A third indicator that a relationship is a partnership is that the partners can point to intentional strategies they have developed together to decide on the aims of their joint work and the problems they will solve. Such strategies might include the use of advisory boards, strategic planning meetings with different stakeholders at the table, and meetings where research findings are collaboratively discussed. In chapter 3, we will describe concrete strategies potential partners can use to define aims, negotiate problems, and identify shared values. For now, it's important to know that these strategies differ from traditional contracts, subcontracts, and teaming agreements where one side sets the terms of the agreement. In most partnerships, the strategies used to promote mutualism are jointly conceived and implemented. (See Tools and Templates, exhibit 2: "Deciding What Kind of Collaboration You Want and Need.")

TYPES OF RESEARCH-PRACTICE PARTNERSHIPS

For education leaders and researchers considering forming a partnership, it may be useful to know about different models or types of RPPs. These types of partnerships differ not only in the strategies they use to promote mutualism, but also in the roles that researchers and educators are expected to play in them. Some roles and ways of working together are likely to be more attractive to some partners than others—either because of the dispositions and expertise of the partners or because of the aims of the work. Therefore, we present these as "thinking tools" for partners in search of the right organization for them.

There is likely no single best model of an RPP. Rather, the best partnership is one that allows the particular group of people and organizations that have come together to work effectively toward improving teaching and learning outcomes. In some cases, the form of the partnership may even be a hybrid of the different types we describe here. No doubt, there are times when a partnership design is inappropriate, either because participants are not bought into the design or have concerns about their ability to fulfill their expected roles. Last, an appropriate design doesn't guarantee partnership success, because improvement efforts in complex educational systems are challenging undertakings that require ongoing adaptation to a host of dynamic contextual factors.[1]

Today, there are three broad types of partnerships: research alliances, design-based research-practice partnerships, and networked improvement communities. In this section, we describe these types of partnerships and give an example of each.

Research Alliances

Research alliances are partnerships between educational systems and research institutions formed to investigate the policies, programs, and needs related to learners in those systems. They are *place-based* partnerships; that is, they are linked to specific jurisdictions, such as a school district or city. What distinguishes research alliances from other types of partnerships is that researchers study district policies and programs but are not involved in designing them. This is in part because researchers in research alliances seek to serve as independent voices that provide objective evidence regarding educational policies and programs' implementation and efficacy. At the same time, their commitment to being "place based" entails being accountable to educators and community members, as well as maintaining an ongoing relationship with the district. Structurally, most research alliances bind researchers and educators together through formal memoranda of understanding that spell out what work they will do together. In addition, many alliances have boards—whose members come from educational organizations, teacher associations, parent and community groups, and research organizations—to help set a long-term strategic vision for the alliance.

The coupling of the desire to maintain independence with the long-term commitment to work together in a particular place creates some possibilities as well as tensions that must be managed in research alliances. An important possibility is that the research alliance can serve as a powerful outside voice for stakeholder groups that are represented on their governing boards, groups who may represent students and families from nondominant communities. For this to work, though, educators must allow researchers to report truthfully about the effects of programs and policies, whether or not they are effective. Researchers have to learn how to share bad news with educational leaders so that their ongoing relationship is not damaged. They may even need to withhold broader sharing of results that educational partners deem too risky to share, in order to preserve the integrity of the partnership. Alliances often focus on a district's most sensitive issues, so navigating political pressures is essential to partnership success.

Even though research alliances are focused on studying local problems, policies, and programs, they do share findings beyond their local settings. They create policy briefs to inform national conversations, and they publish their findings in academic books and journals. In order to publish their findings in peer-reviewed journals, research alliances must maintain academic standards of quality. For many researchers in alliances, however, conducting rigorous research on the impact of programs and policies is part and parcel of their commitment to districts, so meeting academic standards of quality is not something they do only in order to get published. Rather, leaders of alliances argue that adhering to rigorous research design standards lends greater external credibility to the work, which in turn adds to researchers' internal credibility with district stakeholders.

To perform their analyses, research alliances typically rely on a mix of administrative data from districts and data they collect or assemble. Examining the effects of policies and programs on data that the district already collects and maintains for accountability purposes—such as student test scores—is important, because these outcomes matter most to educational leaders. At the same time, in order to help the district to understand patterns of change and stability in teacher and student outcomes, research alliances may collect data on school contexts and policy and program implementation. Researchers organize the data from different sources into archives that they use to perform analyses. The archives may include longitudinal data on individual schools, teachers, and students, and may link disparate datasets from districts and even from community-based organizations. Creating an archive can require complex data-sharing agreements that researchers and educators carefully negotiate at the outset of the partnership and that partners periodically revisit.

An example of a research alliance is the Baltimore Education Research Consortium (BERC). Launched in 2006, BERC is a partnership of the Baltimore City Public Schools, Johns Hopkins University, and Morgan State University. The research partners in BERC conduct and share analyses both of learners' needs and of policies and programs, with the aim of informing decisions about policy and practice. As in other research alliances, BERC researchers strive to provide an independent voice, contributing to ongoing improvement efforts within both the schools and the community.

Also as in other alliances, BERC has a formal governance structure that helps maintain the responsiveness of its research agenda to the concerns of school officials and the community. An executive committee guides BERC's overall strategic direction. Its members come from the universities involved in BERC, Baltimore City Schools, and a number of civic organizations. A memorandum of understanding with the Baltimore City school board lays out BERC's organizational structure, agreements for sharing data with researchers, and the broad scope of its research agenda.

BERC has conducted multiple studies of district policies and programs, spanning a wide range of district topics. For instance, BERC has conducted studies examining attendance patterns in early elementary grades, diagnosing how early attendance problems lead quickly to students falling behind in school.[2] Researchers from BERC have also studied the effects of various out-of-school time initiatives.[3] Most recently, BERC has examined the college readiness of Baltimore City Schools students.[4]

Design-Based Research-Practice Partnerships

Design-based research is a form of educational research that is similar to engineering research, in which ongoing feedback cycles inform improvement. In separate articles in the early 1990s, psychologists Ann Brown and Alan Collins first described the approach as arising from their frustrations with laboratory studies of learning.[5] They found that laboratory studies were very hard to replicate "as is" within classrooms, an observation that has been made many times since. Brown and Collins called for a "design-based" approach to developing and testing learning interventions in real classrooms. Design-based research uses an iterative, theory-driven approach to classroom testing, in which researchers first seek to embody theories in specific tools (e.g., software), materials (e.g., curricular activities), and practices (e.g., routines for classroom discussion) and then study the use of these tools, materials, and practices as they are implemented.[6] Today, design-based research is used widely for early-stage research and development projects.[7]

As applied within RPPs, one form of design-based research is called Design-Based Implementation Research (DBIR).[8] Where most design-based research focuses on testing in only a handful of classrooms, DBIR focuses on testing innovations in a large number of classrooms, such as across a district. DBIR also involves iterative design and testing of supports for implementation of classroom innovations. Thus, DBIR efforts are informed by theories of policy implementation and organizational change. In DBIR, the focal problems are jointly negotiated among researchers and educators, who then collaboratively design solutions to those focal problems.[9]

The direct involvement of researchers in the design process is one element that distinguishes design-based RPPs from research alliances. The researchers do not seek independence from their partners, nor do they assume a stance of objectivity. Rather, they work collaboratively to apply theoretical perspectives and empirical evidence related to learning and organizational change to designing solutions to district problems. And while design-based research can lead to programs that can be tested in random assignment studies, the developers' primary focus is on continuous iteration to optimize implementation and outcomes and to develop new knowledge about how to organize conditions for particular forms of learning.[10]

An example of a design-based RPP is the Seattle-Renton partnership with the University of Washington, in which Dan is a leader. This partnership is funded through a state grant (a Math-Science Partnership) and focuses on building capacity to implement the Next Generation Science Standards (NGSS), which are based on current research in how students learn science and were first published in 2013.[11] Because the new standards call for fuller student engagement in science and engineering practices, and for assessments that test students' grasp of these practices, implementing them is likely to require major shifts in teaching practice.[12]

The partnership is led by science curriculum leaders from two districts and researchers from the University of Washington's Institute for Science + Math Education led by Philip Bell. Dan is the principal investigator of the grant and guides the evolution of the work to build his district's capacity to implement the NGSS. The co-design work has centered on teacher professional development customized to align with available curriculum materials at each grade level. Early in the partnership, the team designed professional development to prepare teachers to engage their students in writing explanations of scientific phenomena and building and using models. The partnership has also addressed, for elementary teachers, curriculum adaptation as a strategy for preparing teachers to lead equitable instruction in science.[13] Teachers took existing units from the adopted district curriculum and integrated into them opportunities for students to engage in explanation, argumentation, and modeling. More recently, the work has expanded to include preparing teachers to design classroom assessments that measure all three dimensions of science proficiency emphasized in the NGSS—disciplinary core ideas, science and engineering practices, and crosscutting concepts.

The University of Washington researchers involved in design activities also conduct research on partnership activities. In addition to examining changes in teaching practice, they document the growth of a network of teachers who share partnership resources with colleagues in the school district. Researchers have developed social network maps that demonstrate the spread of resources throughout the school district. The maps have helped Dan secure ongoing support for partnership activities from his own supervisors.

Networked Improvement Communities

Like design-based research-practice partnerships, networked improvement communities (NICs) design and test solutions to problems of practice, but NICs are different from design-based partnerships in other respects. NICs are a new form of partnership in education, championed by leaders of the Carnegie Foundation for the Advancement of Teaching.[14] In a NIC, a network of educational organizations forms to address a specific, persistent problem of practice, and collaborates to design and test solutions using a specific set of methodologies adapted from medicine for the improvement of key routines in medical practice.

Though this form of partnership is relatively new in education, the idea of harnessing the power of a network to guide improvement efforts is not new. The software engineer and inventor Douglas Engelbart coined the term "networked improvement communities" to apply to groups engaged in collective pursuits to improve a capability, such as that of schools to provide effective teaching and learning opportunities to students.[15] Engelbart saw great potential value in bringing together a group of people and organizations concerned with the improvement of some core practice—not just to share what they had learned and test strategies together—but also to investigate how to improve their own work processes. Thus, a NIC is not just about improvement, it is about "improving improvement."

In a NIC, the roles of researcher and educator are intentionally blurred. Everyone is a contributor to the improvement effort, and educators typically play a central role not only in designing and testing strategies for improving practice but also in collecting and interpreting data. More salient to a NIC are the defined roles of *hub* and *network node*. The hub brings together people from practice and research who have the necessary expertise to engage in the work and to organize specific improvement efforts. Facilitators in the hub require expertise in the methodologies of improvement science, including how to design and test change strategies, how to gather evidence related to the effects of change strategies, and how to build a network around a shared understanding of the problem they are trying to solve. Participants in the network node relay with hub facilitators to contribute to the endeavor ideas specific to their expertise, to pitch in to help design, implement, and gather evidence related to change strategies. Because few, if any, strategies work the first time, network participants are also expected to help iterate on designs and test revised strategies in their work.

In contrast to both research alliances and design-based research partnerships, the members of NICs are not always part of the same educational organization. In this respect, they are not place-based in the same way that other types of partnership are. A good example is the Building a Teaching Effectiveness Network (BTEN), formed by the Carnegie Foundation for the Advancement of Teaching to address problems of beginning teacher retention and development. BTEN comprises leaders and teachers from two different school districts, a national teacher association, a charter management organization, the Institute for Healthcare Improvement, and Carnegie, who together served as the network's hub. Carnegie staff served as facilitators of the network hub itself.

The methods used in NICs for negotiating focal problems of practice and for designing and testing innovations are adapted from fields outside education. For example, some processes and tools used to identify root causes of problems, such as using Plan-Do-Study-Act cycles to examine "small tests of change," come from industry and business management practices developed initially by W. Edwards Deming. And the method for slowly and deliberately bringing improvements to scale—by assembling strategies that prove to be effective across a wide range of contexts into a "change package" that others in the network can use—comes from approaches developed in health care.[16] Applying each of these methods in the context of a NIC requires some specialized expertise, and the Carnegie Foundation for the Advancement of Teaching is a primary source to which nascent networks turn to acquire this expertise.

The form of research that takes place in NICs is also different from research in other types of partnership. Unique to NICs is an emphasis on *practical measurement*—that is, a form of studying whether improvements work in the context of educators' ongoing, daily work.[17] In practical measurement, the purpose of measurement is to serve the improvement effort directly, not to hold educators accountable or yield reliable measurement evidence for the purposes of publishing social scientific studies. Practical measurement has its own set of requirements that make it a systematic form of inquiry, even though it does not follow modern traditions of psychometrics precisely. For example, in practical measurement efforts, measures are continuously refined to increase the likelihood that observed variations in practice strongly predict outcomes that the NIC is focused on improving.

Carnegie's work with a different network, comprising community colleges, to improve the outcomes of students in developmental mathematics illustrates well the unique nature of partnership work within a NIC. This particular NIC was formed around the aim of dramatically improving the pass rates of community college students who were placed in remedial or developmental mathematics courses when they enrolled. Students assigned to developmental courses must complete them before they can enroll in courses for which they earn any credit toward a degree, but those same students are the least prepared and often face other challenges (e.g., financial pressure, balancing jobs and family obligations with coursework). As a result, they may spend a whole term or even year in college, drop out without passing the prerequisite developmental courses, and leave without a single degree-counted credit. As part of the early stages of NIC formation, the team brought together leading community college mathematics educators who had been successful in helping students build the competencies needed to pass developmental mathematics courses, and researchers specialized in curriculum and mathematics learning. Carnegie staff, in collaboration with external researchers, conducted multiple "scans" of literature related to specific topics, such as what the NIC would come to call *productive persistence*—that is, students' ability to develop skills and maintain positive mind-sets, an idea that comes from the writings of psychologist Carol Dweck.

These scans informed what in improvement research is called a *working theory of practice improvement*, the NIC's best current understanding of what it takes to accomplish its aims. To represent that working theory this NIC used tools of improvement research, namely a "driver diagram" that represents the best thinking about what primary and secondary drivers of change are, as well as the NIC's "best bets" about where and how to intervene to improve the percentage of college students receiving college-level credit for mathematics within one year of matriculation to community college.

The team applied Plan-Do-Study-Act cycles to test specific improvement strategies in a variety of dimensions related to the NIC's focal problem of practice—improving the outcomes of community college students in developmental mathematics. For example, they tested strategies for improving productive persistence through multiple cycles. As part of the iterative cycle of testing, the team conducted two small experimental trials and—in less than six months—was able to transform an abstract and novel idea into a concrete intervention that could support the NIC's goal in a wide variety of classrooms. Key to the effort were a set of practical measures implemented and refined as part of the tests. What made them key was the discovery of a single indicator—students' report that they felt a sense of *belongingness uncertainty*, a heightened sensitivity to the strength of their bonds with others in the academic setting within the first weeks of the semester—that strongly predicted persistence and grades at the end of the semester. This discovery helped the team refine its focus for developing and testing strategies to improve productive persistence, and the team credits the discovery with helping increase the percentage of students earning college credit in mathematics after a year, the principal aim of the NIC.

Hybrid Forms of Partnership

Not all partnerships fit neatly within the typology we have presented here. For example, in the past several years Regional Education Laboratories (RELs), contracted by the US Department of Education as support providers to districts and states, have been tasked in their contracts with forming research alliances in their regions. These research alliances resemble the kinds of place-based alliances described earlier, but their geographic scope varies more widely and their relationship to the US Department of Education shapes their activities in ways that differ from those alliances. One such difference is that the US Department of Education requires that RELs' reports undergo peer review before being released publicly, a process that can be lengthy. Although the report drafts are available to research alliances much earlier for their use in decision making, the timeliness of public reporting has been a challenge for these alliances.[18]

An example of a Regional Education Lab partnership is the Northeast Rural Districts Research Alliance. This alliance comprises districts across New England and upstate New York and is led by Pam Buffington, a facilitator at the Education Development Corporation. The alliance conducts descriptive and correlational studies on topics of importance to alliance members, and it also includes technical assistance focused on data use. One of the equity issues that is challenging for rural districts to address is access to higher-level courses. The alliance has conducted descriptive studies of rural students' use of online courses in algebra to better understand how and when students access this content. The alliance is also focused on helping bring conversations about data into the community. In many rural areas, schools are a central hub in the community, and so the alliance focuses on studying strategies that bring conversations about school performance and efficiency into the community. It is also exploring how to link community health indicators and educational indicators to improve student outcomes.

Another example of a hybrid RPP is one between the Clark County School District in Nevada and SRI International. The partnership includes leaders from the district's Curriculum and Professional Development and research offices, as well as science education researchers from the Center for Technology in Learning at SRI International. This partnership, funded by the Institute of Education Sciences' Researcher-Practitioner Partnerships in Education Research program, is primarily focused on improving understanding of the needs of emerging bilingual and multilingual students (English language learners) in elementary science. The SRI researchers are conducting original analyses of data on ELLs' language proficiency and science achievement to better understand the challenges they are likely to face when encountering the discourse-intensive practices of explanation, argumentation, and the development and use of models in science emphasized within the Next Generation Science Standards.[19]

This partnership has several features of a research alliance but also some important differences. As in alliances, the researchers integrate multiple datasets with district administrative data to perform independent analyses. The researchers explore relationships between fifth-grade students' science test scores in English language arts and mathematics, and whether those relationships vary by student ethnicity, gender, or free and reduced-price lunch status. The researchers also conduct interviews with principals and school-level science leaders to learn how teachers plan and implement science instruction in their classrooms, how they differentiate instruction for emerging bilingual students, and how they access and use the curriculum resources. The goal of these research activities is to help the district refine its understanding of the likely challenges emerging bilingual students face in meeting the new state science standards, much as a research alliance helps districts to develop understanding of focal problems of practice.

At the same time, this partnership also engages in activities that are more typical of design RPPs and networked improvement communities. The leaders say that they are applying the "core principles of Design-Based Implementation Research and Improvement Science."[20] Indeed, the leaders are engaged in a collaborative design process that attends carefully to the inclusion of diverse stakeholder groups, draws on learning sciences research to inform the design process, and employs rapid cycles of testing using a Plan-Do-Study-Act cycle. In this partnership, the involvement of researchers goes beyond what researchers would typically do in an alliance in that they help the district design and test strategies for addressing the needs of emerging bilingual students in science, rather than just studying how district programs and policies operate.

In the case of this particular partnership, the hybrid design fits with the broad aims of the partnership, which are both to understand the needs of emerging ELLs *and* to support their participation in discourse-intensive practices emphasized within the new science standards. The alliance-like activities support one part of the goal, while the design-based research and improvement science methods support the other part.

EQUITY: A CROSSCUTTING DIMENSION OF RESEARCH-PRACTICE PARTNERSHIPS

From improving college readiness of students from nondominant groups to preparing emerging bilingual students to meet new science standards, improving equity is an underlying goal for each of the partnerships featured in this chapter. Though equity may not be explicitly foregrounded in every discussion of partnerships, many partnerships seek to improve educational systems. Whether those systems are districts or learning ecosystems that encompass schools, families, and community-based organizations, inequity in opportunity and outcomes often emerges as a central problem of practice. Data on disparities associated with income, race, gender, and disability status readily present questions to partners about how these disparities persist despite ongoing efforts to address them.

Concerns for equity also inform some partnerships' attention to including diverse voices in defining aims, negotiating problems of practice, and articulating common values. In contrast to traditional research and development activities that are driven by researchers' concerns, partnership research is often designed to reflect the concerns of many different stakeholders in education, from families to community members and teachers. In the next chapter, we explore ways that partners attempt to make good on the promise of equitable participation in partnerships.

3

Learning About Potential Partners

Weighing whether or not to form a new partnership is a little like dating: things will go much better if you get to know your potential partner before you decide to commit to a longer relationship. The "dating" process for research-practice partnerships is a way to get to know one another, as individuals and as organizations with distinct but potentially overlapping aims and values. At the end of this phase, each partner should be able to confidently answer questions about the other, like, "What is Dan's district's biggest challenge to implementing standards?" and "What are the most important research questions Bill is tackling these days in his science education research?" The partners should be able to name some of the things they have in common, as well as the differences they will have to learn to live with as partners.

First, even before you spend time getting to know a potential partner, ask yourself whether a partnership is the most appropriate type of relationship to pursue. It may be better for the researcher to approach a district honestly, not as a partner but as a site for data collection. Or the district might approach researchers to propose a consulting agreement for specific services. Nothing is inherently good or bad about different arrangements; they each suit different purposes. In this chapter, we begin here, with a few concrete tips for figuring out whether a partnership is a good idea for a given situation. Then, for those cases where a partnership could be worthwhile, we provide some ideas for how to organize initial meetings that can get a partnership off to a good start.

The norms, ways of talking, and practices of researchers and educators are quite different. Specific and intentionally designed strategies can help bridge these gaps. These include things like meeting agendas, templates for describing root causes of problems, and research plans. All of these tools help partners determine how they will work together and help establish shared processes in the work. It can also be useful to establish some norms for the partnership to follow. It is important that you and your partners develop a process together for defining clear aims, specifying focal problems of practice, and articulating shared values. Such processes are important especially early on in partnerships, helping people who don't know each other well innovate together by creating some familiar patterns of interaction across different organizational cultures.

FIGURING OUT THE APPROPRIATE RELATIONSHIP

First of all, if the goals of the work are not negotiable, the conditions are not right for a partnership. Each partner must be willing to have the aims of joint work at least partly shaped by the other partner. For a researcher wishing to test an intervention or program, it's sufficient to have an agreement with the district that allows the researcher to conduct a study as long as it doesn't harm the students and employees of the district. Because in this case the researcher specifies the intervention to be used, how often and for how long, and who will participate in what type of data collection, a partnership is not appropriate. The district may benefit from participating in the study—if, for example, teachers receive professional development in a program that proves effective—but the benefit to the district may be only serendipitous.

Sometimes a district has a clear goal for work it needs done and seeks researchers to carry that work out. In those instances as well, a partnership relationship is not a good choice. For example, Bill was recently approached by a district to replace a professional development provider who wasn't available to support the district when it needed. The focus of the professional development fit his expertise—helping teachers understand how to realize the vision of *A Framework for K–12 Science Education*, the National Research Council report that laid out a structure for what would become the Next Generation Science Standards, in their science teaching.[1] The district leaders had already recruited thirty teachers to participate, set dates for the professional development sessions, and had specific goals for what teachers would learn. Bill agreed to lead the professional development as it had been outlined rather than propose another, more jointly defined approach. He coplanned and co-led it with district leaders, and the district paid him as a consultant.

The preceding examples reflect real needs of researchers and districts. So they beg the question: When is it ever a good time to partner? In this section, we discuss some of the supporting conditions of a partnership that can help answer this question. A partnership can be appropriate when educators and researchers share an interest in working together but do not have immediate goals or objectives for joint work. That might sound strange, but it happens often! Imagine that a new district administrator wants to take on certain initiatives over time in her new role, and contacts a researcher she knows who might be a good partner. Or a researcher moves to a new university in a new area, and calls up a district leader who is in a similar position to a leader he's worked with in the past to explore a new relationship. Educators and researchers might learn about each other at a conference or workshop they both attend, develop curiosity about the other's work, and explore working together. (See Tools and Templates, exhibit 3: "Identifying and Recruiting Research Partners.")

Another good impetus for a partnership is when districts know they want to develop capacity to do a new kind of work themselves—for example, addressing the needs of multilingual students or reducing racial disparities in suspension rates—but they need help from an external research partner to do so. In these instances, the district doesn't want just an expert to lead professional development once for teachers or leaders, but rather an outside partner to help them design a professional development program that the district can rely on its own leaders to provide. Or, the district wants the researcher to provide a model that the leaders implement and adapt to their own needs, along with some coaching and ongoing support as the district adapts that model.

In such cases, if the district is willing and able to integrate what the partner is offering, and the researcher has relevant, complementary expertise and shows flexibility in how they will work with the district, a partnership may be possible. Caitlin Farrell and Cynthia Coburn describe this condition as *absorptive capacity*, a useful idea they have adapted from organizational studies to RPPs in education.[2] Absorptive capacity, as they define it, refers to the ability of an organization to make productive use of what an external expert can provide toward its improvement.

There are a number of dimensions of absorptive capacity that are likely to matter for effective partnerships, such as whether there is strong internal communication among those in a district who will need to coordinate work related to the partnership. First, sufficient resources must be invested to support the work, whether provided through partnership activity or by the district. Second, external partners must have the knowledge or skill necessary for the work and be able to communicate effectively to district partners what they know and can do. Third, there must be sufficient opportunities for the partners to interact with one another, in order to transfer knowledge and skill from researchers to district leaders. If all of these conditions can't be met, a partnership might not be worth the investment in time and resources of those involved.

In exploring partnerships, prospective partners need to be wary, too, of how the introduction of external expertise will affect relationships inside the organization. For example, Jon Supovitz's study of a partnership between Duval County Public Schools in Florida and the National Center for Education and the Economy (NCEE) shows that the expertise of the external partner can unintentionally undermine the authority of district leaders to guide reform efforts.[3] In that partnership, district leaders came to realize they could not produce quality materials needed to guide reforms—even though that had been their goal—to build capacity through NCEE to lead whole-school reform according to the NCEE model. That put the district in the difficult position of having to cede authority back to NCEE for coaching and supporting implementation of reforms, a key role the district had sought to play. Partners can avoid this by engaging regularly about roles and how they need to transform over time as partnerships mature, a topic we take up in chapter 7.

THE WAY IT USUALLY BEGINS: A POTENTIAL PARTNER APPROACHES ANOTHER

Though two potential partners may find in a chance meeting that they have something in common on which to build a partnership, it is more common that an educator or researcher approaches the other about a specific idea for collaboration. It won't be clear from the outset whether the collaboration will ultimately take the form of a deeply engaged partnership. On the one hand, coming to a first meeting with a fully fleshed-out proposal for a project can foreclose the partner's chance to shape the project and can thus undermine a partnership orientation. On the other hand, jumping too early into a full commitment to each other's goals is not likely to work out in the long run. So how do you begin?

If you are the one seeking a partner and have some idea of how you might like to collaborate, our first piece of advice is to plan ahead for two initial discussions. In the first meeting, you may state the reason you have asked for a meeting—a grant proposal opportunity or a new district policy, for example—but it is also important to step back and discuss some more basic questions. For one, you need to explain "why did I approach *you* about this opportunity?" in terms the other person is likely to understand and appreciate. If Bill approaches a district supervisor about an opportunity to study how that district makes decisions about curriculum, he needs to explain why *that* district and *that* supervisor in ways that make reference to the district's strategic priorities and initiatives. (See Tools and Templates, exhibit 4: "Initiating a Partnership Meeting.")

Bill also needs to explain why his team is right for the priorities at hand: What interests and expertise do he and his colleagues bring that leads them to approach this particular district about this opportunity? He will need to explain this by making clear the potential benefits to the district. This can all be done in simple terms, as these examples show:

> I am calling about an opportunity to study district decision making, because I know you all are in the midst of adopting a new literacy curriculum. I am interested in how district leaders use research to make decisions, and I also bring expertise in differences among elementary-level literacy curriculum. There's a specific grant opportunity we might discuss, but first I wanted to

hear a bit more about your process, and see if I can answer some questions for you.

I am with the district's research office, and we're noticing there are a number of researchers from your university who work with us on a regular basis. We'd like to see if we can better coordinate our efforts with these researchers, so we can align them better to our strategic priorities. We're approaching you because you've worked with us closely over the years. We figured you might be able to help us think about how to accomplish our goals. Is that something we might spend some time today exploring?

In both of these examples, the starting place is the clear presentation of interests and expertise the initiating partner brings to the table. There is no specific proposal, and there is no detailed account of the person's professional history, accomplishments, and stature in the field. In this initial statement of purpose, less is more, and direct is best. Also, in both of these approaches, the other person is explicitly invited to respond—to elaborate on a strategic priority of their organization (the first approach) or to participate in another conversation (the second approach).

These same strategies can be applied when you are the one being approached. Ask and listen for why you are being approached rather than another district leader or researcher. Find out about proposed focus areas and the other person's relevant interest and expertise. Tell them your honest initial reactions, whether or not they ask for them. Their response to your reactions is your first clue about whether it might be good to work together. Observe carefully, and note how well they listen and hear you.

The first meeting should be like a first date—a chance to get to know the potential partner, taking care to notice what you say that interests them, and what you say that falls flat. It's a time to listen carefully to what topics get them animated and what topics they may struggle with. As on any first date, if it's going well, you may be open to appreciating what this person brings to the table, rather than rushing to judge their foibles. Also, a little bit of enchantment at this stage can help spark mutual interest in further discussions. Just as the outcome of good first date is mutual interest in a second date, not a marriage proposal, this first meeting shouldn't aim for a formalized partnership agreement. Save discussion of formal agreements for a future meeting. (See Tools and Templates, exhibit 5: "Conducting Introductory Meetings with Potential Partners.")

Toward the end of a first meeting that is going well, leave some time to discuss who needs to be at the table the next time you meet. It's always a good idea to assume that there are people not present who have the authority to say yes or no to a particular opportunity, and sometimes they need to be brought in early to discussions. People with less authority but who have a stake in the work might be important to include as well. A large second meeting may not be advisable, but strategically expanding the stakeholders to include those who are likely to be directly involved in the work can help the planning move forward more quickly.

LISTENING AT THE BEGINNING OF A PARTNERSHIP

For both potential partners, in this first meeting, listening is key—both to finding your way into potential joint work and to building mutual understanding. Listening with an ear for how your concerns and interests intersect with your potential partner's can help you identify shared values that can guide joint work. Listen carefully, too, for differences such as unfamiliar language and acronyms, or practices that you find puzzling. Further, pay special attention to any emotional responses—of confusion, concern, or excitement—to what a potential partner says. Awareness of such reactions can help you avoid judging prematurely a priority or practice whose origins and rationale you don't understand.

Because it is all too human to respond to difference with judgment, we have found in our own work some techniques that help us to listen more effectively in initial meetings with prospective partners. First, inquire with curiosity rather than making statements based on underlying assumptions. For example, a researcher might say to a practitioner, "You say that whatever we have to do together has to improve test scores. Can you say more about that?" Or a practitioner might say to a literacy researcher, "You say you only study direct instruction literacy programs; how did you come to study just these types of literacy programs?" Questions that elucidate the background and context behind short answers can help you better understand the other person's thinking. In our experience, once we uncover the history and purpose of a policy or practice we initially find puzzling, we are more likely to discover common ground or at least some way to find shared purposes for improving education. And when we discover that common ground, we name it. We find that doing so helps signal progress in our understanding of one another and opens the way for next steps.

More broadly, it is useful to keep in mind that both researchers' and educators' activities are so colored by their respective aims and values that the activities become shorthand for those aims and values. In other words, for educators, "standardized testing" has come to mean holding people accountable for improving all students' learning, while for researchers, "randomized controlled trials" stands in for the value of rigor and objectivity in research. In the early meetings of a prospective partnership, it is necessary to reiterate the purposes behind activities, and name the values inherent in educators' and researchers' policies and practices. If we assume we already know those purposes, or if we are content with the cozy familiarity of our own initial judgments, we will miss opportunities to articulate new research questions and potentially breakthrough strategies for educational improvement.

FACILITATION IN EARLY MEETINGS

After some initial meetings, you'll want to plan carefully to establish good meeting processes. Dan likes to say that one of the most important tools in a partnership is a calendar. A person who can help keep track of when meetings are, help identify agenda items ahead of meetings, and communicate the goals for each meeting is indeed an invaluable resource for a partnership. Consistency of communication is critical to building trust within the partnership.

Identifying a person or two who can serve as a facilitator is also a good idea, as well as someone who can help coordinate meetings. In our experience, strong facilitation is an important part of a prospective partnership's early meetings. The facilitator's role in early meetings is to draw out potential convergences with respect to aims, make visible the expertise and interests of potential partners, and highlight potential contributions of partners to some emerging shared endeavor. Listening carefully to what is said in early meetings is key to successful facilitation, but a good facilitator has likely also done some homework on the people at the table or is already familiar with their work. A skilled facilitator knows when to ask for elaboration on a point, understanding that elaboration could clarify an opportunity for someone present. Here, we present a set of strategies for successful facilitation.

In an early meeting, it can be helpful to engage people in activities that make visible what each partner brings to the situation and that help to build relationships between individuals. One strategy Bill has used in the past is to play a game he calls "Social Bingo." The game depends on getting some basic background information on participants who will be attending a meeting and creating bingo cards featuring those facts. The facts are typically a mix of personal experiences (e.g., "I've lived in another country") and professional expertise that will be relevant to the work (e.g., "I have led professional development with elementary teachers"). It is especially useful to include on the cards experiences that educators might have had in conducting or participating in research studies or that researchers have had as educators. This makes clear that you prioritize developing shared understanding and can help people see that they have more in common with one another than they might have initially anticipated.

A second facilitation strategy is to revoice participants' contributions to check for understanding. Revoicing is a simple but powerful move when you are working to develop shared understanding in a group setting.[4] Here's an example from a recent early meeting of an educator and a researcher who were considering working together:

> **Researcher:** What do you see as some of teachers' needs that could be addressed through professional development?
> **Educator:** From my visits to classrooms, I see a need for supporting more student discourse. I still see a lot of emphasis on teacher talk or teacher-student talk, but not much student-student talk.
> **Researcher:** So you see a need for supporting more student-driven discussion, where students are really addressing each other's ideas, right?
> **Educator:** Yes, we'd really like students to build off one another's ideas, to develop skill in argumentation.

In this exchange, the researcher doesn't repeat what the educator has said, but rephrases it slightly and even extends it: "students are really addressing each other's ideas." Importantly, though, the researcher invites the educator to assess his interpretation. The educator responds and elaborates on both her own statement and the researcher's. The result is that both gain a sense that they are on the same page and also develop a more refined understanding of the needs to be addressed through their work together.

A third important strategy is to ask people to elaborate more on ideas and practices than they are in the habit of doing in everyday exchanges with colleagues. Acronyms, shorthand ways of describing policies and programs, and academic terminology all require exploration. Sometimes a reference is made to a key initiative in a district or organizational practice in universities (e.g., a tenure and promotion case) that can easily be taken for granted or glossed over. A facilitator can play an important part in highlighting such habitual references and in elaborating on their meanings. "Policing" participants' contributions is not necessary, but requesting elaborations and explanations gently helps people begin to recognize when they are speaking in a way that their prospective partners might not understand. It also helps them to make use of their own language in a more reflective, rather than reflexive and unconscious, way. Of course, noticing when people are speaking in shorthand can be hard when people do not know each other well. It helps when facilitators have had some history interacting with one or more people from each organization in the room and have strong credibility within their own organization.

In addition to strategies they can employ, successful facilitators probably share a few key characteristics as well. One of these is experience—and a certain level of comfort—spanning boundaries among organizational cultures. Organizational sociologists call someone who has close ties to people outside their organization and who enjoys high levels of respect within their own organization a *boundary spanner.*[5] A boundary spanner has learned the other group's specialized language, conceptual frameworks, and social practices, and is thus in a better position to help interpret messages that could be misheard across the boundary between two organizations.[6] Having a boundary spanner present in early meetings of an emerging RPP can be valuable because, for most researchers and practitioners, the other's world is opaque. A facilitator who spans boundaries is more likely to see connections between individuals' interests and link participants' contributions to one another and to the larger goals of each organization than is a facilitator who lacks this trait. (See Tools and Templates, exhibit 6: "Developing Empathy for Partners.")

Many RPPs get off the ground without a boundary spanner, but over time the boundary-spanning role can be a factor in a partnerships' longevity. We will explore more how such roles can be cultivated in chapter 4, when we discuss the important task of building infrastructure in partnerships.

DIGGING DEEPER TO DEFINE AN INITIAL FOCUS OF JOINT WORK

After some initial meetings, most emerging partnerships take some time to find their way into actual work. This way-finding period requires systematic efforts to understand better the nature of the problems that are to be addressed together, to map the educational systems where the work will take place, and to identify the shared values that will inform the search for solutions to district problems.

Specifying Problems

A key early task of partnerships is to specify the nature of the problems that partners will work on together. It is hardly ever the case that the very first formulation of the "problem" will be a most productive one around which to design the joint work. At first, the language used to describe the problem usually comes either from the world of research or from the world of practice, and it is not recognizable to the prospective partner on the other side. Further, the initial problem representation typically represents only a partial view of the situation. A joint exploration of the nature and dimensions of the problem is often necessary before the partners undertake work together, to ensure that their work will reflect a deeper analysis of the problem's context.

One way to undertake such work is through *rapid ethnography.* This is a set of techniques for learning quickly about the recurring patterns of activity and meanings of a group, with the intent of using that knowledge to inform design of some innovation.[7] In rapid ethnography, members of a design team interview prospective users of a product, or those implementing an innovation, to understand their current practice. They may also observe those people as they go about their day-to-day activities.

Rapid ethnography can sometimes truly transform partners' understanding of the problems they set out to address. In the early 2000s, Bill undertook a rapid ethnographic study with colleagues at SRI International and leaders in a small southeastern district that was exploring the use of handheld computers to support classroom assessment. The team initially thought it needed to help teachers who were already well versed in using computers for project-based instruction learn the functionalities of the wireless handheld devices to assess student understanding. But interviews and observations indicated that computer access and wireless connectivity were not reliable, despite significant district investments in hardware and infrastructure in school buildings. Moreover, Bill and his team saw strong evidence of deficit views of African American children who came from one region of the district. It manifested in the ways teachers talked about students and in the ways that people throughout the district talked about that area of the county. As a consequence of the rapid ethnographic study, the team's sense of the problems it needed to solve shifted to include more basic problems of technology integration and racial inequities in how students were treated in school.[8] Note that this is a hallmark of RPPs—the initial ideas about the problem to be solved change and expand as a consequence of mutual engagement.

There are other ways that partnerships can refine their understanding of problems that become the focus of their joint work. In a partnership between researchers at the John W. Gardner Center for Youth and Their Communities and the town of Redwood City, California, a combined analysis of administrative datasets from schools and the foster care system led the partnership to raise the community's awareness of the challenges foster children face in keeping up academically. Analyzing two sets of extant data in combination sharpened the focus on ensuring these youth received the services that would help them succeed in school.[9] The analysis highlighted especially the need for more services for youth living in group homes and other nonfamily settings. In networked improvement communities, teams map the causes and effects of an observed problem in "fishbone" or "Ishikawa" diagrams, so named because they look like the skeleton of a fish and come from Japanese manufacturing.[10] Working collaboratively to identify the causes of a problem illuminates the complexity of a given problem space for both researchers and practitioners.

Mapping Systems

A clear map of the system that is producing the pattern of outcomes that partners see as problematic can be key to understanding the complexity of a problem. Taking time to learn how to "see the system" as a whole can be an important early activity in a partnership, because people inside the educational system may have little time to step back and reflect on the key system components, interactions, and mechanisms that contribute to undesirable outcomes. Similarly, researchers outside the system may know little, if anything, about a given district's organizational structures and processes. Stepping back can help district leaders see that problems do not persist simply because individual policies fail or individual leaders have shortcomings, but rather as a result of a network of policies, practices, and people that is maintained and supported through multiple (and often relatively stable) routines. For the researchers, mapping the system that produces a pattern of outcomes helps them gain appreciation for why things are the way they are and, hopefully, get a sense of the constraints leaders face in addressing focal problems. The effort of mapping systems reminds us that merely asking people to do better does not make them do better; to improve outcomes, we must change the system.[11]

There are different ways to map the interactions that produce a particular pattern of outcomes. One systematic method that we find useful for partnerships is the *Change Laboratory*, a process developed by Yrjö Engeström and colleagues at the Center for Research on Activity, Development, and Learning in Helsinki, Finland.[12] A Change Laboratory entails researchers bringing together a group of professionals in a particular field (e.g., health care) to form a design team around a focal problem of practice that the group feels the need to address.[13] These researchers typically conduct observations and interviews to identify contradictions within and across different levels of systems, and they present their findings to their fellow design team members. Using the research as a basis, the design team then develops its own analysis of the contradictions in the system that present "double binds" to participants in the activity system—such as conflicting goals to pursue.

A key tool for identifying double binds is a generic template for characterizing an activity system (figure 3.1). Partners can discuss and complete this template together to help them understand how a particular activity

Figure 3.1 Template for analyzing an activity system

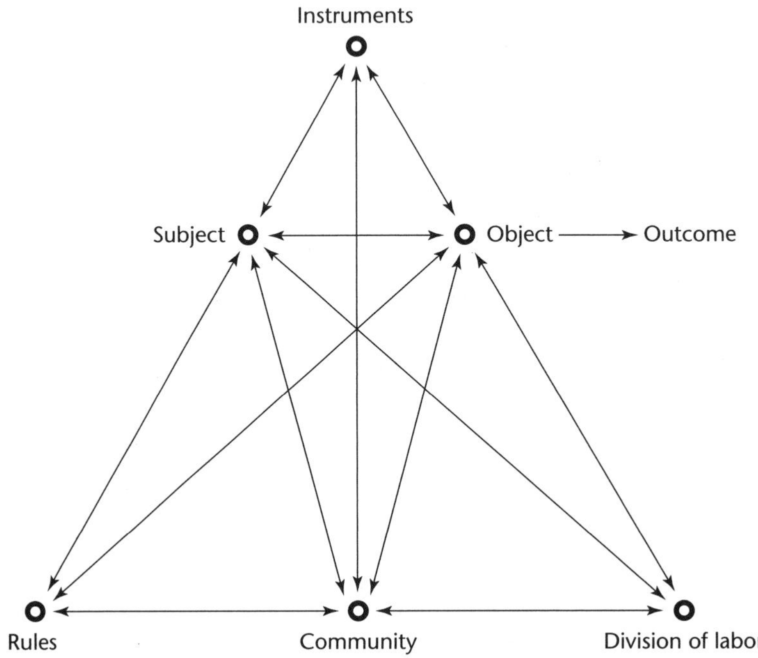

Source: https://en.wikipedia.org/wiki/Activity_theory#/media/File:Activity_system.png.

system produces the outcomes it does. The boundaries of an activity system are defined by the design team engaged in the Change Laboratory; for example, it could be the system of activity that produces patterns of tracking in a high school, or the system of activity that produces achievement gaps in test scores.

As shown in figure 3.1, on one side is the individual, or subject, with his or her own purposes for engaging in a given activity system. This is where different purposes, motivations, and experiences of participants are accounted for. On the other side is the object—what, collectively, all the participants in the system are aiming to accomplish. The outcome and object (aim) are distinct, in order to draw attention to the fact that what is being mapped is an undesirable outcome that is produced. Instruments, at the top of the diagram, are the means by which actors seek to accomplish their aims. In education, instruments might include curriculum materials, district policies, assessments, instructional models, routines for assigning students to special services—anything that could be seen as an instrument or tool for supporting action. Activity systems are also defined by rules, community norms, and a formal division of labor—who does what in the system, in terms of their formal roles.

Along any one of the arrows connecting two or more components of the system, there are often contradictions or conflicts. A subject (individual) may find that the rules that she must follow to develop lesson plans are contradictory to guidance given in adopted curriculum materials (instruments). Or, a division of labor within schools that limits opportunities for teachers to plan collaboratively may inhibit the development of community norms of sharing lesson plans and teaching strategies, which schools may be trying to cultivate in order to promote more collegiality and relational trust.

An example of a successful Change Laboratory in a school setting comes from Annalisa Sannino, a researcher at the University of Helsinki, who was asked by a school principal to provide professional development on formative and summative assessment.[14] She proposed to facilitate a Change Laboratory instead, and the two agreed. In the initial phases of the Change Laboratory, a different focus for the work was established: teachers found it difficult to manage their classes while conducting the traditional individual oral assessments required of all students in the school. Initially, some teachers resisted addressing this problem at all, but through the analysis of tensions within the system, eventually "a different way of talking about change emerged," one focused on making changes together to move beyond traditional forms of student assessment.[15]

Another example comes from the work of Lisa Yamagata-Lynch and Sharon Smaldino, who used an activity system analysis to analyze problems in a partnership among a preservice teacher education program in a university and nine school districts.[16] The two researchers provided specific guidance in helping educators in the district and university-based researchers engage collaboratively in a theoretically motivated analysis of their partnership. The result was the surfacing of new issues and initiation of a search for new solutions to enduring partnership dilemmas. The researchers also documented an important benefit—the more equitable participation of all partners in diagnosing the partnership's difficulties.

Depending on the nature of a problem, it can be valuable to map the system from the standpoint of a particular type of actor within it, in contrast to the approach just discussed, to better understand the specific challenges of those in that role. The Building a Teacher Effectiveness Network (BTEN), the NIC focused on improving teacher retention introduced in chapter 2, did precisely this. BTEN studied all the different sources of guidance and feedback to new teachers in a school, to understand better the nature of the guidance. What they discovered was a cacophony of voices, pointing new teachers in dozens of different directions. Mapping the voices and guidance that were creating confusion for some teachers led BTEN participants to work to better coordinate messages to teachers through the building leader. In many schools partnering in BTEN, this step, along with a protocol for interaction for the leader to use, helped improve teachers' sense that they were supported in becoming effective teachers.

Identifying Shared Values

The role of shared values is central in RPPs. A shared sense that participants are working toward the same aims for students, and with a common commitment to a particular way of working together, can help partnerships face the inevitable setbacks with courage and resolve. Conversely, discovering that you do not share a common commitment to equity or to building teacher capacity with a partner can undercut the search for solutions and make it difficult to find one's way into joint work.

Recently, colleagues at the Exploratorium formed a network called the California Afterschool Tinkering Network with support from the National Science Foundation. At the start of this network of museums and afterschool programs, the group had decided to focus on equity in making and tinkering activities, but the participants realized they did not have a shared definition of equity to guide their work. On the one hand, concerns about equity had brought everyone together, along with interest in fostering an emerging practice at the intersection of art, science, and engineering learning. The group organized a meeting to discuss the meanings of equity through a "value-mapping" activity. Each participant put meanings on sticky notes, and the participants together elaborated on their notes, asked questions of each other, and then grouped the notes into clusters that seemed to reflect different aspects of equity that were important to the group. Following that exercise, the network used the resulting map in subsequent meetings to guide decisions on research questions to pursue and to set agendas for meetings. (See Tools and Templates, exhibit 9: "Promoting Equity Within a Partnership.")

The value-mapping activity didn't just identify shared ideals, it also revealed key differences among members of the group that became topics of subsequent discussion. According to two leaders of the emerging partnership, Jean Ryoo of the Exploratorium and Emily McLeod of Techbridge, "For us, the Value Mapping activity surfaced the different ways members understood learning to occur through STEM-rich tinkering, how we as a group defined equity for afterschool education for non-dominant youth, and where our ideas overlapped or differed."[17] One disagreement that the mapping exercise surfaced was the role of scientific vocabulary in making and tinkering activities. Some participants thought scientific language was important for promoting equitable access for students, but others thought expecting familiarity with specialized language too early would create unnecessary barriers. As the group's work progressed, the team's efforts to identify strategies for equitable facilitation in making and tinkering activities reflected an appreciation of these different perspectives.

BEYOND MECHANICS: WHAT THESE STRATEGIES ENABLE

While this chapter has focused concretely on strategies to support the building of a partnership in the early stages, underlying all of them is a commitment to organizing partnerships so as to enable partners to leverage one another's experiences and expertise. (See Tools and Templates, exhibit 7: "Are We a Partnership Yet?") These strategies set a foundation for mutualism that is essential for partnership, and they enable the partners to begin to learn together and do things they couldn't do in isolation. The implementation of these ideas is likely to generate excitement, confidence, and trust, as well as a sense of possibility. In the next chapter, we focus on a concrete set of strategies for building an infrastructure for partnerships that can support more, and more ambitious, joint work.

4

Building an Infrastructure with Tools and Routines

Most readers will agree that researchers and educators have quite different professional norms, vocabulary, and practices. Partnerships, in our view, benefit from having some specific tools and routines to bridge these differences, especially early on. By "tools," we mean things like meeting agendas, templates or diagrams for describing root causes of problems, and research plans—concrete aids that partners can follow, complete, or otherwise use to determine how they will work together. "Routines" are repeated sequences of activity that people in organizations follow. Partners can develop routines for defining clear aims, specifying focal problems of practice, and articulating shared values. While it is true that any routine can outlive its usefulness, routines play an important role in partnerships: they help people who don't yet know each other well innovate together by creating some familiar patterns of interaction across different organizational cultures.

Tools and routines are the core infrastructure of a research-practice partnership. We mean a few different things by the term *infrastructure*, and each meaning speaks to an important aspect of getting a partnership under way.[1] For one, infrastructure enables people to work together efficiently. Just like the system of pipes through which water flows when you turn on the faucet, infrastructure in a partnership assures those involved that resources for a given task stand at the ready. Strong infrastructure makes transparent certain aspects of working together: you already know what processes and resources can support a new line of work.

Relationships—among people, practices, tools, and routines—are also part of the infrastructure that girds partnerships. Relational infrastructure includes both relationships between the partners and the professional ties of each partner to his or her respective organization. A good working infrastructure for an RPP is one in which the partners' joint work—carrying out a research study or designing a new assessment system for a district—is recognized as a vital activity within each partner's organization. A good working infrastructure is one in which the products of the partnership can find "homes" within the worlds of both research and practice. For education partners, that might mean that when research is produced by the partnership, there is a routine in which researchers present and discuss findings with stakeholders in the study. For research partners, it might mean that study findings are regularly published in peer-reviewed journals or presented at conferences to other researchers. The infrastructure of a partnership builds on existing relationships and institutions and connects the networks of people and practices of partner institutions in new ways. The process of building such an infrastructure is slow going. It is intensive and it is incremental. Building infrastructure is some of the hardest work in a partnership—and some of the most important.

FORMAL AGREEMENTS ABOUT HOW PARTNERS WILL WORK TOGETHER

Sooner or later, many partners realize that they need some kind of formal arrangement that specifies how they will work together, how they will make decisions, and how they will allocate resources within the partnership. A grant proposal early in partnership development, for example, requires decisions about who will serve as lead for the grant, how the proposed project will be managed, and how funds will be shared among different organizations for the proposed work. Partner organizations enter into formal contracts with one another, if the grant is funded. Sometimes, these decisions happen quickly because of looming grant deadlines. Ideally, the partners will take time to carefully consider what arrangements are best for protecting the mutualism of the partnership. (See Tools and Templates, exhibit 8: "Who Should Be at the Table?")

Mutualism works differently in different contexts. Sometimes, deep historical inequities and exclusions inform decisions about how partners will work together. Megan Bang and her colleagues describe the agreements that she negotiated as part of a partnership among Northwestern University, TERC, the American Indian Center (AIC) of Chicago, and different organizations on the Menominee reservation in Wisconsin.[2] The team jointly acknowledged that historically both education and research have been controlled by people outside Native communities, undermining these communities' sovereignty and portraying Native peoples in a negative light. With this historical context in mind, the team made a purposeful decision that indigenous people would fill the majority of leadership roles in the partnership. The group also committed to pursuing participatory research that would include "teachers, elders, parents, community experts, researchers, and youth in all aspects of the research, including the conceptions of the problems, project design and implementation, and data collection and analysis."[3] The partnership also includes opportunities for Native American graduate students to conduct research. As the partners established ways of relating to one another that respected the contributions of all stakeholder groups and recognized ways that past engagements had harmed indigenous communities, the team viewed these core elements of the partnership as crucial to promoting and maintaining mutualism.

Another teaming arrangement that reflects a deep commitment to mutualism is evident in the agreements that the John W. Gardner Center for Youth and Their Communities makes with its partners. As in the example of combining data from school systems and the foster care system discussed in chapter 3, the Gardner Center works closely with several communities to develop "youth data archives," databases of information about youth outcomes in multiple sectors, from housing to social services and education. In that respect, the Gardner Center is similar to research alliances that build data infrastructures to perform analyses on a wide range of topics related to their partners' problems of practice (see chapter 2). But Gardner Center researchers use their data infrastructure to build both knowledge and relationships with communities. To maintain strong relationships, the researchers agreed that community partners had a say in how their data was used and with whom findings would be shared:

> Each agency that contributes data helps identify the research questions, interpret results, and review analyses before publication. No analyses are done without explicit approval of an agency representative, and agencies may remove their data from the YDA [Youth Data Archive] at any time. Agencies also help decide how results will be shared and in what format. With permission, we may share findings with other partners, publish and post briefs online, or disseminate to the broader research and policy community.[4]

Of course, not all researchers in research alliances subject themselves to such conditions, but nearly all have something akin to what the University of Chicago Consortium on Chicago School Research calls a "no surprises" rule—namely, that they do not release findings before partners have reviewed them.[5] In this way, alliances help protect the relationships they are building with partners, even as they sometimes confront partners with difficult data—evidence of a failed policy or program, for example, or evidence of a problem that educators didn't know existed.

More broadly, when partners are crafting a formal agreement, it is valuable to assume that historical inequalities are in play since there are structural inequalities not only among groups of people but also among institutions. In the realm of educational decision making, state and local education agencies have tremendous authority to effect changes, more so than parents, community members, and outside researchers. And relative to teachers, school and district administrators have more say regarding policies on the allocation of teachers, students, and curricular resources to classrooms. At the same time, outside researchers may have greater status than educators and the ability to bring in resources in the form of grants, which they can control. Teams must take these inequalities of power, status, and authority among different stakeholder groups and institutions into account when organizing for mutualism in partnerships. (See Tools and Templates, exhibit 9: "Promoting Equity Within a Partnership.")

In some instances, researchers have partnered with community members rather than educators with formal leadership roles in an educational system in order to overcome inequities. Researchers at the University of California Los Angeles's Institute for Democracy, Education and Access formed the Educational Justice Collaborative (EJC) to organize for equity in California schools. This group's work is premised on the idea that educational opportunities cannot be equalized through efforts entirely within the educational system; promoting equity requires bringing together youth and community organizations to organize for change.[6] The EJC partnership has been successful not only in engaging young people in participatory inquiry into opportunities in their schools, but also in bringing about new policies to remedy opportunity gaps the partnership identified. For example, in the early 2000s, the EJC joined forces with advocacy groups in the region to make college preparatory course requirements the standard curriculum for all high school students in Los Angeles.[7]

Another example of such a partnership is the Denver School-Based Restorative Justice Partnership (DSBRJ), a collaborative effort among representatives from several organizations focused on addressing racial disparities in discipline. The partnership comprises a parent and youth group called Padres y Jóvenes Unidos, a national racial justice organization called the Advancement Project, the Denver Classroom Teachers Association (DCTA), Denver Public Schools (DPS), the Graduate School of Social Work at the University of Denver (DU), and the National Education Association (NEA). The grassroots efforts of Padres y Jóvenes Unidos and the Advancement Project first drew attention to racial disparities in Denver's discipline practices to the district, resulting in DPS's adoption of new discipline policies.[8] Those new policies led to a dramatic reduction in overall rates of suspension of students of all backgrounds, but—as researchers in the partnership documented—racial disparities remained and so became the focus of efforts to foster more equitable implementation of DPS policies throughout the district. At present, this partnership is working to develop a more robust intervention support system within the district, grounded in the work done in three different DPS schools.[9]

PARTNERSHIP GOVERNANCE AND DECISION MAKING

The degree to which partnerships have formal governance structures varies, but successful partnerships need some well-specified routines for making decisions. Many research alliances have advisory boards that provide significant input from community members and advocacy groups. These boards help shape the groups' research agenda, and they also provide support for alliances to publish findings that can put pressure on school districts in the way that the EJC did. Design research partnerships tend to have more informal governance, with design projects' goals and key actors influencing partners' approaches to decision making. In networked improvement communities, once partners come together around a focal problem, governance is led by a "hub" that directs improvement efforts with input from practice structured through improvement science methods. In this section, we present examples of different approaches to governance in partnerships and describe what each affords its partnership.

Governance in the Baltimore Education Research Consortium

The Baltimore Education Research Consortium (BERC) is a research alliance modeled loosely on the University of Chicago Consortium on Chicago School Research. When BERC was formed in 2006, its aim was to bring together university researchers, district leaders, and representatives from community organizations into a mutualistic partnership that was similar to the Chicago consortium but reflected the "political, social, and historical realities of Baltimore."[10] As noted in chapter 2, BERC is a partnership among the Baltimore City Public Schools, Johns Hopkins University, Morgan State University, and several Baltimore nonprofit agencies. It grew in part from a number of successful smaller partnerships between Johns Hopkins researchers and Baltimore City schools, but from the outset, BERC sought to expand beyond Hopkins to include a local Historically Black University, Morgan State, and other local colleges and universities over time.

Also from the start, BERC had an "executive committee" that would include nine voting representatives—three each from the participating universities, Baltimore City schools, and the community. The "community," early planners decided, could include members of the business community, nonprofit and advocacy organizations, parent groups, or public agencies other than the district. These have included the president/CEO of the Greater Baltimore Urban League, the president/CEO of Associated Black Charities, and the Baltimore City Health Department's Deputy Commissioner for Youth and Families. This committee helps to set the longer-term research agenda for BERC, but it does not decide on specific projects. With this mix of participants, the board ensures that the research is relevant (community input) and rigorous (researcher input). The balance of power is intended to help adjudicate among the only partially overlapping concerns of the district, university researchers, and community organizations.

The initial planners for BERC were concerned about both political interference and inappropriate censoring.[11] Like the University of Chicago Consortium on Chicago School Research, they instituted a "no surprises" rule, agreeing that all BERC reports would first be shared with only schools and other agencies being studied thirty days prior to public release. But the schools or agencies could not stop these reports from being released, nor did they have the authority to stop a study once it was under way.

Decision Making in the Inquiry Hub

The Inquiry Hub is a design-based research-practice partnership that formed in 2011 among researchers from the University of Colorado Boulder, the University Corporation for Atmospheric Research, and Denver Public Schools. Bill is a leader in this partnership. The Inquiry Hub brought together people and ideas from two separate research projects, focused on using digital tools to support more student-centered teaching in mathematics and science, undertaken between 2007 and 2011. Initial funding for the partnership's activities came from the National Science Foundation, in the form of a grant from its Cyberlearning Program.[12] The partnership now includes several lines of work (mainly in science education) funded through different sources, including the school district.

As in many other design-based RPPs, many decisions in the Inquiry Hub revolve around what focal problems of practice design efforts should address. The Hub's "leadership tier," made up of researchers and district leaders from the partner organizations, is responsible for these decisions.[13] The leadership tier meets in person on a semiannual basis to discuss the district's current needs and priorities and possible grant opportunities, and to clarify key roles of people in each organization for specific lines of work. In addition to the in-person meetings, the group meets once or twice a month via videoconference to discuss progress and challenges. Lastly, all weekly research team meetings also include a member of the district leadership team (currently the secondary science coordinator). This is a unique feature of this partnership in Bill's view.

Collaborative grant writing serves as a secondary context for decision making: when researchers and educators write grant proposals, they work closely together to define the needs to be addressed, the aims of the research, and the design constraints that will affect the research. As an example, the Inquiry Hub recently decided to apply for a National Science Foundation grant to support co-designing interim assessments. This focal topic emerged from the partnership's growing sense that the district needed increased capacity to build "three-dimensional" science assessment tasks aligned to the Next Generation Science Standards (i.e., addressing the standards' three dimensions: disciplinary core ideas, science and engineering practices, and crosscutting concepts). DPS specified the timelines for assessment development that would conform to district protocols, as well as the amount of staff time that could be devoted, consistent with its current investments in assessment development.

Other decisions the partnership makes flow from the prior decisions it has made about the focus of the joint work. When the group decides on a focus, it always creates a collaborative design team that includes researchers, district leaders, and teachers. These co-design teams, called *teacher advisory boards*, have a significant say in the content of design. For example, in a line of work focused on designing a new high school biology curriculum, a team of eight to ten teachers has been working with researchers and district leaders to design and test a set of project-based units aligned to the Next Generation Science Standards. The teachers have been part of the decision-making process to determine the content of each unit and have also provided input into the design process itself at multiple stages. The leadership tier has incorporated many of these changes into the process.[14]

Governance in the BTEN Networked Improvement Community

The Building a Teaching Effectiveness Network (BTEN) began as a set of informal conversations among representatives of the Aspen Institute, the American Federation of Teachers (AFT), and the Carnegie Foundation for the Advancement of Teaching. Initially, these conversations were focused on a desire to form a network, but it took leaders in the group some time to find a focal problem to work on together. It wasn't until they engaged in a number of conversations with teachers around the country that they settled on new teacher mentoring and induction as a problem they could work on together.

At first, the plan was for partners to divide aspects of the work that they would lead, with Aspen working on policy, the AFT identifying partner districts, and Carnegie bringing in partner districts to apply improvement science methods that staff were learning from the Institute for Healthcare Improvement.

Carnegie staff led the development of a driver diagram—a representation of the key levers for change that, in the case of BTEN, were hypothesized to improve the effectiveness and retention of new teachers. They sought input from other partners and from the district on the diagram, which they developed internally to guide the work that reflected their own review of available literature and findings from conversations with field leaders. Carnegie emerged as the overall facilitators of the work—in part because the commitment to improvement science methods necessitated it. Carnegie staff were the only people prepared to implement the methods in the network. A consultative model of partnership emerged, with Carnegie staff leading the way but seeking feedback, input, and advice from partners each step of the way. Senior leaders of the major partners continued to meet monthly, but Carnegie—due to its facilitation and analytic capacities—became the hub of the network, guiding the day-to-day decisions on the ground.

The different district partners made their own decisions about which primary driver to focus their efforts on. Initially they focused on distinct areas, but as one district had some success with focusing on improving principal feedback to new teachers, the other districts moved to work in this area of the driver diagram as well. The intention was for the BTEN network to be driven or governed by what the results showed them about the efficacy of different change strategies, and in one sense, that is what happened—as one site showed promise of success, others followed suit. The approach to organizing the network around the driver diagram illustrates a key aspect of governance through which a network can learn together while still preserving local autonomy.

TOOLS AND ROUTINES FOR BRINGING NEW PEOPLE INTO A PARTNERSHIP

Especially since RPPs take place over several years, some turnover among participants can be expected and should be planned for. New people can bring new life to a partnership, or they can threaten its viability. Therefore, it is important to build in from the start some tools and routines for bringing in new people, as well as for expanding a partnership when necessary to engage in new forms of work. In this section, we describe how different partnerships engage in both of these kinds of efforts.

Bringing New People On Board When Someone Leaves a Partnership

Central-office turnover in a district or reorganization often requires bringing on new people to a partnership. A district curriculum coordinator retires or is promoted to a new position, and a new person steps into the role. Or the curriculum office is reorganized, creating a different set of positions with new roles and responsibilities. In such cases, it makes sense to bring in the new person whose responsibilities align better with the work of the partnership, even though the partnership's former member is still employed at the central office. In both instances, it's necessary to help new people become familiar with the work of the partnership and take on roles within the partnership that fit the current context.

One of the ways that Dan helps induct new Seattle district colleagues to their partnership with the University of Washington is to periodically interrupt the flow of meetings to provide context for participants about what university researchers are saying. For example, if a junior researcher refers to her "tenure committee," Dan might explain how such committees work in the university as compared to K–12 tenure in schools, highlighting similarities such as tenure decisions being highly consequential for university researchers' job security and long-term career prospects.

Dan also debriefs with newcomers after their first few meetings, checking in about what they view as the meeting's takeaway points, to see how they make sense of what people say and do in the meeting. He also helps people understand when an issue mentioned in passing is a pet peeve or a recurring concern for another team member. These strategies help Dan ensure that his staff gradually acquires a sense of where the partnership has been, who its key players are and how to work with them successfully, and how to fit their contributions into the flow of ongoing partnership activities.

Dan also considers empowering district leaders to speak up in meetings and contribute their expertise one of his important roles. University faculty often speak freely, and they may talk a lot and in an authoritative manner. Researchers are also more apt to disagree with other speakers than are educators, who may view such disagreements as personal attacks rather than challenges to ideas and positions being discussed. Dan tries to help teachers and other district leaders see the expertise they bring to the table and to pay attention not just to the strengths of university researchers but also to the gaps in the researchers' knowledge. He sometimes sends a note ahead of time to people saying explicitly, "I am counting on you to speak up in the meeting," as a way to encourage them to contribute. These moves are critical to helping educators feel confident to share ideas in conversations with researchers that may feel unfamiliar and uncomfortable to them.

In partnerships involving universities, graduate students and postdoctoral researchers often take on significant work—leading some design activities, carrying out data collection, and leading data analyses. As these team members complete their studies or postdoctoral positions, they typically move away to begin their next position. More often than not, their work with the partnership ends with their relocation. In a few rare occasions, departing graduate or postdoctoral students remain involved, but the relationship may shift, and new students and postdoctoral researchers need to be brought on board.

One of the ways that Bill helps new students join the Inquiry Hub is by providing them with some core readings to do ahead of time. He focuses on having them read articles that are directly relevant to the work being done, as well as articles about partnerships and approaches to design-based research. He assigns a breadth of readings because he wants new students and postdoctoral researchers to understand how the partnership contributes to research knowledge, and how researchers collaborate in a partnership with district leaders or teachers.

As much as possible, Bill also has new students and postdoctoral researchers read things authored by Inquiry Hub team members about the work of the partnership. This material can include grant proposals, conference presentations, and published research articles. In his view, these readings help people appreciate the partnership's specific history and gain perspective on where it is headed. He wants to avoid students and postdoctoral researchers proposing things the partnership has already done, or that are not feasible given the constraints of resources or district policy.

It is hard to know at first where a new team member's strengths and learning needs lie. Curriculum vitae and interviews are only partly useful to get a sense of a new member's dispositions toward partnership work, potential skill in working collaboratively with educators and organizational leaders, and particular research interests that might be fulfilled through project work in a partnership. So, Bill likes to pair new members with veteran students and research scientists to work in small groups, where they can be mentored actively and partnership participants can get to know them, give feedback on work, and provide context for why the partnership works in the ways it does.

Of course, a new team member may not work out. There is more flexibility in a graduate program than in a workplace, however, when a team member is not a good fit for the work. In such cases, graduate students need help finding their way to projects that better suit their dispositions, interests, and skills. Bill reviews students' fit to the project every semester, and works with colleagues to find new placements for students for whom the partnership is not a match. Bill and his colleagues see their role as university faculty as not just supporting their own projects, but also helping students find their way into work that matches their interests and dispositions. Research-practice partnership work is not a good fit for everybody.

Expanding a Partnership to Include New People for New Lines of Work

It is not uncommon for RPPs to bring on new people with expertise or authority relevant to new lines of work that they wish to pursue. A partnership focused on curriculum design may realize it needs to expand to include assessment design, but there are no measurement experts on the team and the district's assessment office is not a major player in the partnership. Under such circumstances, the partnership has to figure out where to find the needed expertise and how to bring on an additional researcher or new central-office leader into the partnership.

Because new lines of work often require grant development efforts to obtain needed resources, such efforts can be purposefully structured to help identify new participants and bring them into the work. A key preliminary task, though, is to vet potential new participants with partners, discussing candidates' expertise and relevant aspects of their current roles before inviting them formally to participate. Once potential team members join the proposal development effort, it is important to have follow-up meetings and conversations (like those Dan has with new members, as described earlier) to help provide context for what transpires in planning meetings. An important goal of such follow-up conversations is to elicit new participants' understandings of both the partnership's work to date and how the new person can contribute to planned future work.

There are other ways to vet new potential participants in a partnership. In one research alliance, leaders use a set of informal breakfast meetings held regularly with members of the partnership to observe new researchers' interactions. If they are considering bringing on a new researcher to the partnership, they want to make sure first that the researcher has the right disposition and skills for partnership work. They invite that researcher to present or just to come and listen at the breakfast meeting. At these gatherings, leaders look for evidence of clear communication of research findings, as well as respectful listening to practitioners and community members. If candidates show little evidence of either, they might not be invited back or to join the partnership.

Sometimes, when a new team member gets off to a rocky start, work is needed to repair misunderstandings and build stronger relationships among veteran members of the partnership and new members. Bill was recently invited to join a partnership to help conduct some research analyses on data that the partnership had been collecting. He became a remote member of the partnership, along with other colleagues at the University of Colorado Boulder. To accomplish the work he agreed to do, he and his colleagues had to make several requests to developers at another university. But the developers did not have a clear sense of the nature of the new work or why he had been invited to do the work in the first place. They did not appreciate the extra workload, either. It took a trip to meet in person with the whole team—to build relationships and gain clarity on the purposes and nature of the work—to help repair the harm done.

PROJECT MANAGEMENT IN PARTNERSHIPS

One of the biggest challenges in RPPs is synchronizing the work of researchers and practitioners. The daily, monthly, and annual rhythms of researchers and educational leaders couldn't be any more different from one another. Educators' daily work depends on their roles—for example, whether they are a central-office administrator or a teacher. Researchers' rhythms aren't all the same, either. A researcher in a nonprofit organization whose primary responsibilities are all research-related has a different work life from a researcher in a university, who balances research with teaching and service to the department and university. Today, everyone moves quickly, but it still seems to most educators that researchers move much more slowly than they do. All of us drop the ball from time to time. All of these factors can threaten a partnership, not just because they make the task of coordinating joint work more difficult but also because they get in the way of building trust, a key ingredient in a partnership.

Project management is essential for partnerships, especially once they have more than one line of work going at a time, as mature partnerships often do. What is harder about project management in a partnership than in a single organization is that it requires coordination of people and tasks across organizations with very different priorities and rhythms. Partners have to fit their work with each other into their respective workdays while remaining responsive to supervisors and leaders in their own organization. Larger partnerships may have multiple subteams carrying out different tasks on a single project, and they may also have teams working across different projects. Under such circumstances, tools and routines become essential to the functioning of the partnership.

Project management literature is vast and based largely on the wisdom of practice within organizations that are quite different from schools, but it does convey some useful factors that project management in a partnership must attend to. For one, project management entails careful attention to patterns of communication among team members.[15] Along similar lines, project management involves being mindful of group and team dynamics; a good project manager makes adjustments to team composition, workload, and assignments based on how well people work together.[16] It also entails processes for keeping people abreast of what is happening in the partnership, as well as what is happening in the partner organizations that is affecting the work.[17] These include protocols for updating people on teams, including the medium for communication (regular project meetings, a daily or weekly e-mail, etc.). Project management also involves attending to the rhythms of project teams and the flow of projects—knowing when it is time to accelerate work or to slow it down, to foster divergent thinking or move toward consensus, or to focus everyone's attention on a particular matter or allow for side conversations.

All of these dimensions might suggest that project management requires a heavy hand, but this is not necessary, especially if multiple team members take ownership of some aspect of project management. One example of this approach is a project management strategy that the Inquiry Hub tries to follow, originating from software development, called *agile* project management.[18] Agile methods grew out of software developers' dissatisfaction with traditional "plan everything ahead of time" models in which they specified all the software requirements with clients up front and then proceeded to develop the software accordingly. Most business environments—not unlike education environments—are dynamic and constantly changing, and so planning everything ahead of time is a good way to leave clients unhappy with applications that do things they no longer need. Agile methods work from a different premise, namely that one should communicate with clients often and build working products quickly, even if they don't do everything the client needs right away. The users on the client side realize what additional things they need by testing early versions of the application, and the development team works quickly to enhance the prior version to address those needs.

Working in an agile manner actually requires a light touch in managing people. It entails fostering a team environment where people are comfortable sharing their work and their struggles with others as they go, and also working closely with at least one other software engineer on tasks, to produce more reliable software. The manager who tries to lead by controlling people and timelines too tightly is actually in a bad position to adapt as quickly as agile software development demands. Rather, the agile manager sets a few simple rules and norms for interaction and communication, values all team members as skilled and essential contributors to the effort, and minimizes excessive planning for far-off events and circumstances.

Software development is certainly different from project management in a partnership, but in a design partnership like the Inquiry Hub, many aspects of agile project management and development can easily be adapted to the education context. The team tries to work quickly to get new curriculum and assessment resources—which they know will need revision—into the hands of teachers, so that teachers can improve them for the next iteration. When possible, the team pushes small things out quickly—a lesson plan template, a tool for designing assessment tasks—for teachers to try in professional development settings or in their classrooms, in order to get early feedback on them. The Inquiry Hub also works openly, sharing with all members of the team—including teachers—the dilemmas they wrestle with and the design decisions they face. As a result, teachers contribute not just to the products of the design but also to the design process itself, making suggestions that help the team work more efficiently.[19] In this way, the work is both rigorously designed and eminently usable. The Inquiry Hub also assigns people to all tasks in pairs, threes, or fours, rather than having people work alone on tasks, because they find that collaboration increases the quality of work and reduces the frustration that can occur when work falls to just one person. Finally, they reconfigure their teams as needed, when they discover people have different interests or skills than initially anticipated, or when people get excited about something they want to pursue that fits within the overall project goals.

DATA IN PARTNERSHIPS: AGREEMENTS AND ARCHIVES

Original analyses of data are often one of the most important ways that researchers can add value to educational systems and communities. Conducting such analyses, though, requires careful negotiation of agreements regarding how data will be shared, analyzed, and reported. Earlier in the chapter, we described one type of data agreement—between the researchers at the John W. Gardner Center for Youth and Their Communities and the Center's community partners—that is simultaneously broad and restrictive; it allows for sharing of data with researchers from across multiple societal sectors, while it restricts use of those data to analyses related to questions that all partners agree are important. At the other end of the spectrum, the Inquiry Hub, which to date has not developed any comprehensive data agreements, simply uses the existing infrastructure of the university and partner district for reviewing research with human participants to obtain data from the district or collect new data from teachers and students. This approach requires researchers and educators to negotiate the terms of data sharing each time a new study is mounted—which could be anywhere from every six months to every three years, depending on the partnership—which is relatively inefficient.

Negotiating data agreements is something that research alliances often do up front, when they are formed. Often, those agreements are formed with a single organization (e.g., a school district), though some, like the Gardner Center's Youth Data Archive, encompass data from multiple organizations. Data-sharing agreements include a number of provisions that should be expected, given that many of the data shared are protected under the Family Educational Rights and Privacy Act, or FERPA (PL-20 U.S.C. § 1232), which gives parents and legal guardians some control over their children's educational records. To that end, agreements address issues of privacy, confidentiality, and data security. A partnership that has a broad data-sharing agreement may have a type of restricted-use license, and may not have access to any individually identifying information for students, in order to protect parents' and caregivers' rights. Other partnerships may negotiate broader access to data, when they are able to offer greater guarantees for data security. At present, state laws are changing that make data sharing potentially more challenging to negotiate, due to high-profile breaches in data security that put student privacy at risk, so it is important that developing partnerships keep abreast of the laws that apply in their states.

Another important consideration related to data agreements, and to the necessary protection of human participants in research, pertains to the identification of partner organizations and leaders in research. Individuals' confidentiality must always be protected; saying something negative about a program or practice might otherwise result in reprisals. Protecting confidentiality ensures that partnerships get honest, accurate feedback on their efforts, too. As partners, sometimes it may be appropriate for researchers to identify the partner organization, provided there is an agreement in place about when it can be done. For example, representatives from the organization may copresent with their partners at a conference, in which case it is difficult to protect the organization's identity. There are risks to identifying partner organizations, however, when the results of a study do not shed a favorable light on them. For example, a district might not want to be identified in a large study that found that a program it had been invested in did not work. On the other hand, identifying the partner organization may help gain positive attention when reforms are successful. Also, education leaders may identify themselves and their organization when they collaborate with researchers on writing—as Dan did in writing this book with Bill. The identification of both partner organizations and individuals presents a dilemma to researchers, specifically about how best to adhere to guidelines for the protection of human participants. The ethical imperative to "do no harm" by the research must be followed, but figuring out how best to meet that imperative requires explicitly negotiating when to identify and when not to identify partners and their organizations by name.

The payoff for negotiating data-sharing agreements in advance has been significant in a number of research alliances, especially when administrative data is complemented by data collected by researcher partners to address specific questions of importance to the partnership. An example comes from the University of Chicago Consortium on Chicago School Research (CCSR), where researchers conducted a study of the effects of Chicago Public Schools' different teacher induction programs on teacher retention.[20] CCSR drew on district personnel data on retention and a survey it designed and administered, in combination, to generate new insights on the conditions under which mentoring programs helped retain teachers. CCSR was able to do this efficiently because it had already negotiated permission to administer a survey each year to teachers, parents, and students throughout the district and to integrate it with other data in the district.

MEETING AND SOCIALIZING

A cartoon greeting card from the website someecards.com reads, "We will continue having lots of meetings until we find out why no work is getting done." It expresses a feeling we have all had in meetings, namely that if we weren't sitting there, we would be getting our work done. No doubt, this joke speaks to the inefficiency of many meetings, but meetings in partnerships are essential for coordinating complex work across organizations. In addition, they are not just places where people report on work they've accomplished and deliberate on decisions, but important spaces where relationships are developed and renegotiated.[21] Having a good partnership meeting involves balancing efficiency goals—so people can go and get their work done—with building productive relationships.

How frequently should partnerships meet? It depends, but the schedule should be based in part on the nature of the work, how much coordination is required, and importantly, the speed with which the partner organizations or their external environments change. In a school district that reorganizes its central office frequently, or adopts new policies that affect teachers on a monthly basis, frequent meetings are essential just to survive. Of course, such conditions may not even be good ones for partnerships, because research cannot be sped up to match the frenetic pace of change in the district. No matter what the conditions, in our experience, e-mail is a poor communication medium for deliberation and decision making; face-to-face and other kinds of synchronous meetings (e.g., videoconferencing) are critical for building trust, developing new lines of work, and coordinating implementation of policies and programs developed through the partnership.

Our colleague Philip Bell at the University of Washington is fond of saying that a core principle of partnerships is, "socialize, socialize, socialize," a quotation he attributes to another colleague of ours, Nichole Pinkard of DePaul University. They mean that team members need to find the time to get to know each other outside of work, when possible, in order to develop a more multifaceted appreciation for their partners. When people are able to build relationships outside the work as well as within it, greater trust develops, and partners become more comfortable sharing things that are troubling them within the partnership. But the purpose of socializing isn't just instrumental: partnerships require an intensity of human interaction, and socializing is a moment to step back and celebrate the generosity and individuality of each partner in their work to improve opportunities for all children.

In the next chapter, we'll go into greater depth with tools and routines related to design, which for many research-practice partnerships is a lead activity. As with the processes we've described in this chapter for building an infrastructure for partnerships, processes for engaging in collaborative design that promote equity and lead to usable, useful innovations are critical to the success of a partnership.

5

Designing Adaptively Across Levels and Settings

The work of educators—teachers, principals, and central-office staff—is often design work. Initiatives to build subject-matter-focused professional learning communities in schools, interventions to help struggling students, new district policies that expand access to advanced courses, and programs that help young people find afterschool activities related to their interests are all examples of strategies that involve designing and testing solutions. By "testing," we mean systematic efforts to study the implementation and impacts of strategies in order to improve them. Many effective research-practice partnerships are oriented to such design work, employing rigorous approaches to design and test strategies that address focal problems of practice in partnerships.

For both researchers and educators, the focus and methods of design are often new. Many researchers who engage in design work are used to working at the classroom or program level, and while some also design professional development for educators, they rarely design policy guidance or organizational routines. The fate of curricular innovations and the success of professional development both depend critically on their fit within the larger system in which the partnership is operating.[1] Many educators are unfamiliar with iterative, collaborative design methods in which teams work in cycles of designing, testing, and revising innovations, using data on implementation and outcomes to inform the process. Educators often only get the chance to do things once, and often are under tremendous pressure to work at scale from the start, rather than testing innovations first in a small number of settings.[2] In this chapter, we share some practical approaches to organizing *participatory design* methods. We find these approaches useful because they make it easier to take advantage of the diverse and expert perspectives in an RPP, and to reflect on how innovations fit within larger systems, including beyond school and district settings.

The chapter contains examples of what design work can look like in RPPs, and we describe some practical methods for collaborative design. Our examples highlight what is often distinctive about the focus of design within RPPs: designing across levels of a system and, in some cases, across multiple settings in a community. As part of our description of participatory design methods, we offer examples from our own and others' work. It may be surprising at first that participatory design, as a Scandinavian approach developed to elicit more worker input on new workplace technologies, can help us with pressing problems in our schools and communities. But we hope to show it makes perfect sense!

DESIGNING ACROSS LEVELS OF A SYSTEM

Most design work in education today focuses on developing innovations for a single group of people (e.g., students, teachers, or leaders) and on a single level of an educational system (e.g., classrooms or schools). This approach is problematic since educational systems are composed of interrelated people, policies, and processes. Changing one component of the system is not likely to be successful without considering how those directly and indirectly affected by the change will respond, or how the change relates to existing policies or processes. Creating valuable and lasting change through design requires "seeing the system" clearly and, when possible, redesigning components and interactions at one level of the system (e.g., the district central office) so that innovations at another level (e.g., the classroom) have a chance of being implemented well.[3] Any innovation that has the potential for sustainability must be "sunk into" existing structures and social processes.[4]

In most school systems, some key "structures" that must be considered are those that connect directly to how school leaders and teachers organize instruction.[5] These include processes like test design, curriculum adoption, and coaching of students, as well as technologies and supports like interim tests, curriculum guides and materials, assessments, professional development programs, and frameworks for teacher quality. The social arrangements include district central-office organization (i.e., roles and responsibilities of different leaders and their relationships to others), the autonomy granted to school leaders to implement district policies, and the relative autonomy of teachers regarding how to teach.

Teachers orient to some or all of the explicit and implicit guidance they encounter as participants in these processes, as users and sometimes co-designers of technologies, and as people who have to navigate different formal and informal social relationships. How they orient to these messages matters a great deal to implementation: if teachers decide that an innovation conflicts with what their principal tells them they must do, then they may decide not to implement it. By contrast, if they get the same message from district-office leaders, principals, and curriculum guides about what kinds of changes they should be making to teaching, then teachers who buy into the new direction may move quickly to implement those changes. Thus, if a partnership is building a new classroom innovation that a team hopes to spread throughout a district, the team may need to address barriers across multiple structures and processes at the district and school levels in order to promote its broad implementation.

This kind of "infrastructure redesign" is precisely what has taken place in the Inquiry Hub partnership, where Bill and his team have been working with a group of high school science teachers to design new science curriculum.[6] Early in the design work, teachers expressed concerned that the district's pacing guide—that is, a document showing how many weeks should be devoted to different topics—did not leave enough time for all the key concepts in a unit Bill's team was developing. The unit was going to take about eight weeks to implement and was intended to address specific expectations in the Next Generation Science Standards. But the district pacing guide called for just two weeks to be spent on these concepts, at the end of the school year. Fortunately, because the district science coordinator was in the room and was responsible for the pacing guide, the design team could pause their work on the unit to figure out what changes needed to be made to the pacing guide in order for the teachers to feel good about devoting eight weeks to teaching the new unit.

The pacing guide wasn't the only thing that needed adjusting, though. The district also required students to take low-stakes end-of-course assessments in science, and these were tied to the pacing guides. In addition, a different team was developing the items for the tests, and although the tests covered the same topics as the new unit did, they would not adequately capture what students were learning in the unit. The items focused mainly on factual recall, not on students' ability to apply big science ideas to explain a phenomenon in the natural world, as the Next Generation Science Standards called for. So, at the invitation of the district science coordinator, Bill worked with Inquiry Hub colleagues to design some assessment tasks that could be included on the district tests. His concern—shared by some of the teachers on the project—was that if the tests did not align with the unit at all, once again teachers who had agreed to devote a full eight weeks to the unit would not feel justified in doing so.

These were not the only elements of the district's instructional guidance infrastructure that mattered to teachers, either, and the partnership has not always been successful in reshaping components that could threaten the viability of the curriculum. For example, the district has an observation system that uses a protocol for evaluating teaching, and the system relies on principals and peers to conduct observations. The protocol's elements were, in the design team's view, consistent with the aims of the partnership, but the principals and teachers outside science who came in to visit teachers' classrooms didn't always see it the same way. Though the team developed a "crosswalk" tool to help observers see links between what kinds of teaching the new curriculum would support and what was on the protocol, at least one teacher still got a low rating when observed piloting one of the unit's lessons. The research team was able to work with district leaders to troubleshoot the situation as best they could, and the teacher continued to be excited about his involvement in the project.

Sometimes, the partnership design team has had to adjust its own practice, when infrastructure redesign was not an option. When several teachers told the team that their principals required every lesson to start with a "Do Now"—an exercise students could work on independently as soon as they sat down in class—the team had to build these into the unit's lesson plan templates. At first, the team struggled with how to make these "Do Now" exercises meaningful and fit them within the instructional model they were using. Eventually, they converted the "Do Nows" into opportunities for students to reflect on the previous day's lesson and to generate questions that arose for them from that lesson. In that way, the exercises could help strengthen the "connective tissue" between lessons. The team thus reworked an initially annoying requirement to serve one of its key goals—creating coherence across lessons in a unit.

The shift to thinking more about the kinds of infrastructures needed for improvement—rather than thinking about individual programs and practices—has been an important one for the Inquiry Hub partnership. It has helped the design team see more clearly the system as a whole and understand teachers' individual contexts better. It has also led to a stronger partnership with the district's science leadership, because the team has been able to contribute to more aspects of their work. At the same time, it has humbled the team to see just how much building leaders' demands on teachers must be accommodated, especially without broad connections to principals and other departments in the central office. This underscores the need for partnerships to include people with the authority to change multiple policies and practices at the school and district level, in order to create a more coherent guidance system for teachers.

For help articulating principles for guiding infrastructure redesign, the Inquiry Hub team turned to an unlikely field of study—information science. Among other things, information scientists study the ways that different classification schemes and standards for practice get layered into different kinds of organizational structures, such as how categories of diseases and diagnoses get integrated into medical practice.[7] These might be called *information infrastructures*, and one of the principles for studying information structures in organizations is that designers should directly engage with what is already in place in a given system.[8] This may seem obvious, but most designers of educational innovations don't take stock of what's already in place as part of the design process or when planning for implementation. We can imagine that the fate of innovations might be different if designers first looked at how decisions are made in a district, mapped the system's key initiatives and structures, and surfaced contradictions and dilemmas faced by teachers in their everyday practice.[9] A second principle of studying information infrastructures is that change must be modular and incremental; it is not possible to change an infrastructure all at once.[10] That means focusing on key leverage points within a complex system where a focused intervention can have effects that are not limited to a single component of the system.[11] A third principle is that infrastructure redesign needs to be thought of as continuous activity, because infrastructures require constant work to maintain and are in constant motion.[12] A fourth principle is that infrastructure redesign must be participatory, because robust infrastructures require actors from different parts and levels of systems to serve different purposes.[13] Later in this chapter, we describe a set of tools and methods for engaging in participatory design, but first we describe another way design work in partnership can differ from traditional design in education: designing across different learning settings.

DESIGNING ACROSS FORMAL AND INFORMAL LEARNING SETTINGS

Increasingly, partnerships are focusing on strengthening networks or systems of supports for young people's learning across multiple educational settings. There's an increasing appreciation of the need to expand young people's access to high-quality learning opportunities in summer and in the hours before and after school, not only because these are opportunities that allow them to discover and develop interests that might lead to future careers but also because participation in out-of-school opportunities is related to how well youth do in school.[14] RPPs can help by designing pathways for youth to explore and develop interests and making those pathways more accessible.

Those are the goals of a citywide partnership involving community-based organizations, public schools, and researchers called the Chicago City of Learning (CCOL). The partnership has developed a platform for compiling information about out-of-school learning opportunities citywide in order to expand awareness of access to these opportunities for youth and their families. Through the CCOL website, youth ages five to twenty-two can learn about sports, arts, media, and academically related programs that are offered in community organizations, cultural institutions, schools, and online. They can earn recognition in the form of digital badges for participating in programs, completing online challenges, and demonstrating knowledge and skills learned in face-to-face programs. When youth earn badges, they are given suggestions for related activities where they can "level up"—that is, further develop their knowledge and skill in an area of interest to them. More than 150 civic and cultural organizations—including the city's many libraries, parks, and museums—as well as the Chicago Public Schools have listed thousands of unique program opportunities on the CCOL website.

Researchers and designers at DePaul University, led by Professor Nichole Pinkard, have built and maintained the platform that helps youth find out about these opportunities in the CCOL partnership. Importantly, CCOL continually refines strategies for making possibly relevant opportunities more visible to youth by using data on what youth look for on the site, as well as by capturing data about the activities in which they participate. The researchers categorize offerings according to topic, duration, and location, as well as by provider. And they have made use of low-cost geographic information systems tools that present visualizations of offerings across the city, which program leaders can use to analyze the broader learning ecology of programs.

A big focus of the team that Pinkard leads is developing formal pathways that enable young people not just to try out new activities but also challenge themselves to develop new skills in a specific area. Using data from the system on available programs, they have worked with selected community organizations in CCOL to design different pathways related to youth interests in writing, computing, and civic participation. Notably, each pathway requires youth to participate and earn digital badges for accomplishments in multiple programs. The programs are not all located in the same place, either. Some pathways require youth to attend programs in different neighborhoods and to complete challenges online. The idea behind locating programs in different parts of the city is to provide incentives (in the form of digital badges) for youth to explore new parts of the city.

Because youth cannot always get to an opportunity of interest, Pinkard's team is working with several organizations to provide a mobile learning lab to bring programming to them. They are using data provided by Bill and some University of Colorado colleagues to help identify what Pinkard calls "learning deserts"—places with fewer program offerings—to determine where to send the mobile labs.

These kinds of community-wide design efforts, while promising, are also challenging to undertake. In the case of CCOL, community organizations have a mix of incentives and disincentives to collaborate to build pathways for youth. On the one hand, they care deeply about improving the learning opportunities for the youth they serve. But many community-based organizations in Chicago compete with other organizations for funding, and how much funding they get is usually related to how many youth attend their programs, not how many youth they refer to other programs. This is not unique to Chicago, but is endemic to the funding infrastructures for youth organizations in many big cities. A critical need in Chicago, as elsewhere, is methods and tools to surface these kinds of double binds and identify new ways of working together to connect out-of-school learning opportunities and bring youth to them.

CO-DESIGN IN PARTNERSHIPS

The design work of partnerships is necessarily collaborative. Collaboration is needed in part because the problems partnerships address involve multiple structures and processes in systems, and partnership work spans multiple settings. No single person has expertise in, or authority to design or redesign, enough structures and processes to solve partnerships' focal problems. But collaboration is also necessary for another reason: to maintain mutualism in the partnership. People who have a stake in the design work and are charged with implementing some component of an innovation need to have a real say in the design work, and not just as "end users" who only say whether an innovation is feasible to implement.

Collaborative design, or *co-design* as we refer to it here, is a strategy for harnessing the collective creativity of a partnership throughout the design process.[15] We use a definition that Bill and colleagues Jeremy Roschelle and Nicole Shechtman developed for co-design in education:

> We define co-design as a highly-facilitated, team-based process in which teachers, researchers, and developers work together in defined roles to design an educational innovation, realize the design in one or more prototypes, and evaluate each prototype's significance for addressing a concrete educational need.[16]

There are many reasons why partnerships might undertake co-design, and in our view, all are important. First, co-design aims at creating more usable innovations that serve a wide variety of educator and learner needs. If the people who are supposed to benefit from an innovation are involved in co-design, those needs are more likely to come up throughout the design process. Second, co-design can yield innovative solutions that no single designer is likely to devise alone. Despite the familiar stereotypical image of a lone innovator with a brilliant idea (light bulb!), the reality is that many of the workplace tools we use today resulted from a lot of back-and-forth across a big team—and the same is true for educational innovations. Third, and perhaps most importantly for partnerships, co-design helps to realize a commitment to mutualism. Co-design in this sense is an ethical stance: we view commitment to promoting democratic participation in educational change efforts as key to addressing historical inequities in education.[17]

The Co-Design Process

The co-design process begins at the stage when a partnership is defining or elaborating on a problem it wants to solve. Co-design teams take stock of current practices and contexts—what's happening at present that is contributing to the problem, how people feel about the problem, and what might get in the way of people trying to address it by introducing an innovation. This initial stock-taking phase can involve research on the setting; in chapter 3 we described one strategy, rapid ethnography, for learning quickly about settings in ways that can inform the design process.

Co-design never begins with a predefined "solution" to the problem at hand, but neither does it begin with a blank slate. It's useful for a design team to move from initial problem definition to defining a concrete design goal. In a networked improvement community, these goals should provide measurable targets for improving some outcome (e.g., to cut in half the number of students failing developmental mathematics). In design-based RPPs, the aims may be framed as a question and focused on something that both addresses the problem of practice and builds knowledge related to a specific domain (e.g., how can we use small, networked devices to support formative assessment in classrooms?). No matter how specific, the goal should not fully define the solution ahead of time, so as to give the design team a chance to imagine and lay out multiple possible solutions to the problem at hand.

To help a team move from problem finding to creating solutions, co-design has what Bill and colleagues call a "bootstrapping event."[18] A bootstrapping event can be a retreat or workshop where participants build a common understanding of the problem to be solved, define the aims for the design endeavor, and begin to imagine some requirements of a solution to their focal problem. These events can last for a few hours or for several days, and provide for an intensive period of joint work. They build a common sense of purpose and a strong bond among participants. When participants leave the event, they rely on that commitment to one another and their common goals to turn ideas into practical innovations as they return to their day-to-day work.

Strong facilitation and leadership is needed both at the bootstrapping event and afterward. Typically this is what makes co-design not "fully democratic," in that some organization has the resources to facilitate the process and ensure that ideas developed in an initial workshop become an innovation that can be tested in the field. Ideally, the leaders of the process continue to engage participants and consult with them, but they chiefly oversee the development process and production schedule, and guide others' participation in the processes. Partnerships can rely on a leadership team comprising both educators and researchers to facilitate co-design as a way to ensure mutualism in the design process. Nonetheless, promoting an equitable co-design process requires periodic invitations to participants to contribute, not just to the products of design but also to its process.

Methods of Co-Design

Few researchers or educators are trained specifically in techniques and methods of co-design, and yet learning a few "tricks of the trade" can go a long way in structuring successful design work. We need methods for different aspects of the work, from brainstorming ideas to developing requirements for solutions to prototyping them in a workshop. Once the bootstrapping event is over, we need methods for organizing smaller teams to work in a distributed way to develop tools and materials and test them in the settings where co-design participants teach and learn. We also need procedures for deciding what to prioritize when we revise designs to improve them. (See Tools and Templates, exhibit 10: "Deciding What to Prioritize in a Design Iteration.") Of course, as with all partnership work, it is critical that teams employing these tools and methods include as wide a range of voices in design as possible, and attend to how particular methods and tools invite or curtail participation of people from diverse backgrounds and in different types of roles.

Fortunately, there are well-developed methods for each of these phases of work that come from practitioners of *participatory design*. Participatory design emerged in Scandinavia in the 1970s as an approach to promote co-operation between managers and workers in the context of designing new workplace technologies.[19] It has developed over the years into a robust set of methods for engaging people in the collaborative design and testing of both technologies and social processes for interaction. Participatory design has influenced scholarship and practice in a number of fields, including planning and architecture, software development, and *computer-supported cooperative work*, whose insights have informed the design of tools we use every day, like instant messaging and collaborative editors (e.g., Google Docs). We describe some participatory design methods here and provide brief illustrations of how co-design teams in education have used them. Our presentation cannot do justice to the depth and complexity of these practices, however, so we hope that you will seek out the more detailed accounts in the books and articles we reference here. In presenting a broad range of tools rather than deeply investigating a few, our intent is to show just how rich the field is with techniques for structuring co-design processes.

Tools for Ideation

Ideation refers to an early phase of design focused on trying to generate ideas for a solution to a specific problem. Most of us have experienced purposeful efforts to promote ideation in the form of "brainstorming" as a group about a particular topic. Brainstorming can be a great way to get lots of ideas on the table quickly and encourage what designers call "divergent thinking"—that is, thinking that entertains many possible pathways to a problem solution. But as practiced in most group meetings, brainstorming doesn't appear as a systematic method for fostering participation. People talk over each other, frequently interrupting to critique ideas or elaborate on them. A good brainstorm, though, is focused on idea generation, not critique and development.

IDEO, a design firm in Palo Alto, California, has developed the following steps for keeping brainstorming on track:[20]

1. Defer judgment.
2. Encourage wild ideas.
3. Build on the ideas of others.
4. Stay focused on the topic.
5. One conversation at a time.
6. Be visual.
7. Go for quantity.

When brainstorming, the facilitator introduces and explains these rules, and also holds people to them. When someone talks over someone else, the facilitator reminds the group of step 5, "One conversation at a time." And if someone has trouble getting his ideas into words, the facilitator might say, "Draw it!," implicitly invoking step 6, "Be visual."

Brainstorming works well once you have a focused topic to brainstorm about, but sometimes you need a way to get people thinking about different dimensions of a problem or working out multiple possible solutions in parallel. One technique we often use in workshops is something we call the "CILT Process," named after a process used in a multidisciplinary collaborative effort called the Center for Innovative Learning Technologies. In this process, participants begin by nominating some aspect of the problem that they feel passionate about working on. Each aspect is listed on a big sheet of chart paper. People can generate many different aspects to work on at first. Then, participants do a "gallery walk" where they write on the chart paper things that they think a group focused on that problem should address. Facilitators might then ask participants to place "sticky dots" (usually small, colored stickers) on problem dimensions they think are important for the team to address. Finally, participants are asked to commit—by moving to stand near a sheet of chart paper—to a specific aspect of the problem they'd like to work on together.

This particular process can feel chaotic in the middle, but we've used it dozens of times and it produces reliable results. Every time, we get lots of different concerns on the table in the first part of the activity. By the end, we get a manageable number of problem aspects that people are motivated to address through their efforts. Though sometimes important aspects of the problem do get left on the walls in the moment, we have those artifacts to which we can return later in the design process to see if we've addressed the concerns described there.

Scenarios

Scenarios are rich, narrative descriptions of people using an innovation that has not yet been developed.[21] Scenarios typically introduce a set of characters resembling the kinds of people who will be implementing or interacting with the innovation, and depict these characters using a tool or participating in a designed activity in a specific situation. Ideally, the situation reflects an understanding of the setting and people's work with it, though the process of developing scenarios usually highlights for design teams where they can improve understanding about the context in order to produce a usable and useful innovation. The interactions specified in a scenario demonstrate how participants make use of a design to solve a focal problem or accomplish goals that the design is intended to support. Describing interactions helps designers to gain different perspectives on the consequences of particular design decisions and features.[22] An additional benefit of scenarios is that, by relying on the everyday language we use to describe human actions—goals, plans, sequences of action, tools, and contexts—they enable people with diverse expertise to contribute to the design process.[23]

Scenario development came in handy for Bill and his team on a complex project focused on supporting instructional coaches for preschool teachers in Head Start.[24] Their task was to facilitate design work on a computer-based tool to document coaching interactions. The design team was composed of a group of early-childhood researchers with expertise in coaching, Head Start coaches, Head Start teachers, and leaders from the National Center for Quality Teaching and Learning from the University of Washington. The group had never worked together before, and although this was not an RPP, the group was committed to co-designing the computer-based program. The scenarios the group members developed for the tool's potential use surfaced a number of issues that had not come up in their initial conversations. For example, they discovered there were many different models of coaching that teachers might be using, which prompted questions about whether or not to design the tool to support interactions within those different models. In addition, data privacy needs were complicated by the fact that many coaches served both as teachers' coaches and direct supervisors. Surfacing these tensions helped the team refine its requirements for the tool and develop features that protected privacy while also providing coaches and supervisors with useful information.

Design Charrettes

A design charrette is an intensive, collaborative experience that brings together stakeholders to develop a shared understanding of the diverse needs a design must meet, and to brainstorm possible ways to address those needs directly through design. Design charrettes bring people together around a single issue typically, and last anywhere from a few hours to a few days. The key is that they are intensive efforts to stimulate creativity among a diverse group of stakeholders, in order to generate plans or designs of greater complexity than can be developed in a brainstorming session. During the sessions, people may build paper prototypes of material tools and technologies, play-act different scenarios, create models of social processes, and imagine creative ways to synthesize ideas about solutions to the issue at hand. The most successful efforts bring people from different stakeholder groups together in a focused way and also seek to develop some consensus around solutions to problems that meet different and even divergent needs.[25]

A good example of a charrette comes from a partnership between the Hive Research Laboratory and the Hive Learning Network in New York City. The Hive Research Laboratory is made up of a team of researchers from New York University and Indiana University that provides research support for the more than eighty out-of-school learning organizations that make up the Hive Learning Network. A key focus for the Network is expanding digital learning opportunities across the city and helping young people navigate those opportunities in a way that allows them to discover new interests and deepen existing ones. One topic that emerged as a common interest of the Network was how adult leaders and family members might better help youth find and access new program opportunities.[26] Network members call this activity *brokering*, a name chosen to call attention to and directly address the well-documented inequities of access to opportunity that are related to social class.[27]

Members of the Hive Research Lab decided to invite Network members to a design charrette to help crystallize thinking about how to better broker youth access across out-of-school opportunities. The members of the Lab knew there would likely be challenges with any such effort, because brokering is time-consuming and depends on educators' and family members' awareness of opportunities that might be available and a good match to youths' interests. The charrette engaged participants in exercises to identify the "who" of brokering—that is, which adults could and should serve as brokers across settings—as well as the "what" of brokering. In the charrette, participants generated several practices of brokering, including helping youth register for programs and creating opportunities for youth to expand their skills by becoming teachers in a program. The research team used these data to create a model of brokering, and they developed a report for the network that not only summarized the ideas generated but also included examples of brokering among Hive Learning Network members.[28]

Design Sprints

Design sprints are a time-intensive part of a broader toolkit of agile development methods. As described in chapter 4, in agile development, users are involved regularly in the design process to provide feedback, but they are not always on design teams. However, a sprint—an intensive effort that involves designing and testing a high-fidelity prototype of a tool—can involve key stakeholders in a partnership, provided they have the time to invest. Where a charrette might last only a few hours, a sprint might last a week or more. Google Ventures has developed a sprint methodology that unfolds over five days. At the end of the five days, a relatively complete solution to a specific problem has been generated.

In an educational context, a design sprint works best when the problem is relatively well defined and when the focus is on the development of a concrete tool. At the beginning of a sprint, the problem is further unpacked, and people begin to imagine possibilities for addressing the problem as they analyze it. Next, participants in the sprint sketch different possible solutions to the problem, discuss them, and then purposefully remix ideas to come up with new ones. Participants then decide on an idea to develop and test during the sprint, spend a day building the prototype, and finally test it with users. During the user test, researchers document how people interact with the prototype and evaluate it against the definition of the problem from the first day.

The Inquiry Hub used a design sprint to develop and test a prototype tool that was intended to fit into a curriculum unit focused on ecosystems. The co-design team had decided it would be useful to have a tool that could help students document organisms and their relationships in their schoolyard. Some of the pieces of the curriculum already were in place, so the tool needed to fit in and support those pieces. A subteam of software developers and educational researchers on the team decided to organize a design sprint to settle on an initial interface and interaction design for the tool. Over the course of the week, the team clarified a number of goals and built a live interface for the tool. The tool had none of the ultimate functionality that would eventually be built for storing images of organisms and tagging them, but the prototype had enough fidelity to allow teacher users to see what it could do in the test. Over the course of two years, this prototype became more and more sophisticated, but much of the current tool's core functionality was specified in the brief time period of the sprint.

User Testing

User testing is a practice in software development for assessing the usability and value of tools for a specific population of people. In a user test, real users try to use a tool or system to accomplish tasks that it is expected to support. Researchers directly observe users, and they typically also interview users about their experiences afterward. A single user test of just a handful of people can identify major problems with a tool; likewise, multiple small tests, in which designers make improvements between each test, can prevent many difficulties associated with using a tool at scale.[29] (See Tools and

Templates, exhibit 10: "Deciding What to Prioritize in a Design Iteration.") In the context of an RPP, "users" could include teachers who were not part of the design team for a tool, as well as students. The co-design team could be the leaders of user tests, responsible for interpreting data from user tests and deciding how to improve the tool.

One partnership that has made extensive use of user testing comprises researchers from two nonprofit research organizations, the Education Development Corporation and SRI International, and a public media organization, WGBH. The partnership, which has lasted several years, builds interventions for preschoolers in the areas of literacy, mathematics, and science that are implemented in schools but make use of games and television programming that children can view at home. From the start, the partnership has faced a challenge in integrating digital tools into the preschool environment: preschool teachers are legitimately worried about providing additional "screen time," during which young children are isolated from peer interaction.

To address this challenge, the co-design team set out to develop some mathematics games that children could play collaboratively on the same tablet computer. The idea was to build a game to support student interaction, rather than put children in front of a screen on their own. The team wanted the interactions to focus on mathematics learning—specifically helping young children to learn the idea of "fair sharing," or distributing a collection of objects fairly. This idea of fair sharing or *equipartitioning* is a foundational skill for developing children's understanding of fractions.[30]

The team's initial attempts at tablet games often presented a number of difficulties for children that were not anticipated by designers.[31] For example, when designing *Photo Friends*, a game in which children work together to share items fairly among characters in different scenes, designers anticipated that young children would have difficulty using the camera to photograph items for characters. But this proved to be easy for the children. The main challenge was to figure out how to keep them from avoiding the intended learning goals; the team needed to design the game such that children had to pause to reflect with a peer on incorrect answers in order to resolve them. Over two years and multiple rounds of testing in three different states, the design team was able to cull fifty prototype applications down to eight that children could use easily and that supported their learning goals.

The Politics of Co-Design

Engaging in co-design is always partly going against the grain of how educational reform efforts typically unfold. It is more common for policy makers, local leaders, and researchers outside the classroom to devise policies and programs for students that teachers are expected to implement with fidelity. It is rare for teachers to have a say in those policies and programs, and even rarer to engage young people themselves and community members in the process. Politics are always part of co-design, because co-design is about shifting the balance of power toward more democratic participation in the process of improving education.

The particular politics that live within the co-design process depend in part on who is at the table in the process. Within co-design projects in which teachers and school or district leaders are present, differences in authority and tensions between these two groups may be particularly salient. In addition, those assigned to key roles need to have status in the group as respected leaders and experts; otherwise, people may not line up to support those charged with moving design work forward. In multiorganizational partnerships, tensions between schools and community groups may arise, in part because of the constituencies these different organizations represent. Community groups often represent people with less power and who have been excluded from conversations about the direction of school reform. In such instances, co-design facilitators need to be aware of and make room for difficult conversations, where relations begin from an adversarial stance.[32] (See Tools and Templates, exhibit 11: "Defining Leadership Roles in Design.")

Researchers are also necessarily implicated in these politics. When a school district insider assigns a leadership role to a researcher from outside the organization, for this shift in authority to work, the researcher needs to have credibility and status with the people in the co-design process. The researcher needs to have credibility with members of her own team—so that she can marshal the necessary resources inside her own organization to carry out the work—as well as with educators. Researchers' identities as outsiders and as "experts" can shape the dynamics of relationships and the process of co-design in ways that sometimes amplify the voice of teachers or district leaders, or play a mediating role between the two groups.[33] Other aspects of researchers' identities, such as race, gender, sexual identity, and class, are relevant to the politics of co-design as well. Sometimes researchers find themselves aligned with different participants in the design process because of their own identities—for example, because they were once teachers in a district or are members of the same community as those organizing for change. Those alignments can reinforce inequalities or can challenge unequal power dynamics, depending on the role the researcher plays and the dynamics of the design process. Researchers should approach the design process expecting existing social inequalities to shape the dynamics of co-design, even though co-design is intended to be inclusive and participatory.

Describing these dynamics in partnerships, Sapehr Vakil and colleagues discuss the need for a *politicized* trust to exist in partnerships.[34] They suggest it is not enough to talk about relationships in terms of mutualism and trust without also speaking to dimensions of power that exist in our relationships, even when we intend to share power. All of our relationships are shaped not only by our individual history but also by the history of our society. No one enters into partnership without these histories, and it is far better to anticipate ways they may show up in the dynamics of co-design than to pretend they don't exist. Remembering that trust has a political dimension that comes into play when people design together is critical to structuring a process that attends to historical and recurring inequalities.

In the next chapter, we address a set of issues closely related to the politics of co-design: maintaining partnerships in the face of turnover, changing priorities within organizations, and the inevitable ups and downs of partnership relationships.

6

Expanding Joint Work and Relationships in Partnerships

Partnerships need to be able to thrive in fragmented and unpredictable environments. The American educational system has many different actors in it, each with distinct goals and ideas about how to improve teaching and learning. Every actor, moreover, operates within multiple policy environments. School, district, state, and federal policies all influence what teachers do in the classroom, and these policies often provide incoherent guidance that changes in irregular cycles. Partnerships need to be aware of the larger landscape of actors and policies in the systems they serve, and need to know when to adapt to and when to attempt to influence their changing environments by expanding the scope of their joint work.

The vulnerability of partnerships is illustrated by the turbulent history of whole-school reform models in the 1990s and early 2000s. These models—exemplified by well-known instructional programs like Success for All—enjoyed considerable policy and funding support beginning in the early 1990s. Schools serving primarily low-income students could use federal funds from several different sources to purchase these programs, and the private foundation New American Schools invested significant funds in selected models' development and implementation in several major school systems A number of external partnering organizations, especially Success for All and America's Choice, grew their staff significantly to accommodate the rapid growth of programs in schools needing support for implementation.[1] By the early 2000s, moreover, there was some emerging evidence of the success of these models in improving student achievement, when models were well implemented.[2]

Despite these successes, little is left of the whole-school reform movement, because policy changes associated with the federal No Child Left Behind Act of 2001 resulted in a shift toward districtwide reform initiatives and away from school-level reform models. To survive, organizations like the Success for All Foundation and America's Choice adjusted course, creating "menus" of services that districts and schools could adopt.[3] They also took advantage of new funding for experimental research in education, pursuing and winning research grants that solidified the evidence base for their programs' reform strategies.[4] In 2010, the Success for All Foundation won a large scale-up grant that was funded through President Obama's Investing in Innovation (i3) initiative, helping the group sustain its presence in a large number of elementary schools. Even so, this was not the future that leaders of whole-school reform models had expected.

While not research-practice partnerships, the cases of Success for All and America's Choice are instructive for maturing partnerships, especially those involving school districts. Any partnership between an educational system and an external organization must be able to survive amidst constantly evolving conditions. In addition, partnerships' success is always dependent upon outside actors—policy makers, investors, and leaders—whose actions affect the partnership's ability to grow and carry out its work. Partnerships that are nimble and adaptive, as well as those that cultivate relationships with outside actors who can provide support, are ones that can be sustained over the long haul. But contingencies are unavoidable, and strong relationships are necessary to weather the inevitable difficulties that arise within the work. Also, partnerships lack formal authority in most cases, making it difficult for them to create policies and allocate resources needed to mitigate threats to their survival.

In this chapter, we describe strategies that partnerships can use to survive in uncertain and often challenging environments. In some instances, partnerships must adapt to the environment around them, but in other cases, maintaining integrity to their principles demands that they directly engage with forces and people that potentially stand in the way of their success. Direct engagement requires strong, diverse, and trusting relationships, which are likely to emerge as partnerships mature, as well as expanded capacities for coordinating more complex work.

FRAMING PARTNERSHIP WORK: WHAT TO EXPECT

To some people, research-practice partnerships are mainly a means to an end: getting ideas from research into practice. They believe that practitioners can more readily implement research findings about what works if researchers are around to help them access, interpret, and use research evidence to guide their decision making. In fact, there's some evidence to support this notion: sustained interactions between researchers and practitioners do facilitate the use of research evidence.[5] But that's not all that RPPs are, and it's not a terribly useful way to think about partnerships, which are not a one-way street from research to practice but rather a relationship in which each party strongly influences the other, as in a healthy long-term relationship between two individuals. (See Tools and Templates, exhibit 12: "Ways Partners Can Support Each Other's Work.")

One of the longest-standing RPPs between university researchers and out-of-school organizations is the Fifth Dimension in San Diego. Initiated by Michael Cole and colleagues at the University of California, the Fifth Dimension is an afterschool club for students, a volunteer resource for community organizations, and a practical laboratory for university students to learn about and apply cultural theories of human development and learning.[6] The design of Fifth Dimension calls for undergraduates to work side by side with children, and play is a primary means by which adults and undergraduates work together to support children's learning and development.[7] Undergraduates are expected to try different ways of relating to youth and to record their reflections in field notes, where they relate their experiences to theories they are learning in a class on campus. Over the years, there have been dozens of Fifth Dimension programs, though over time, the activities of the after-school clubs have evolved. At the beginning, computer-based games were a primary activity, while today many Fifth Dimension sites have embraced making and tinkering activities of the kind found in many makerspaces.[8]

One of the Fifth Dimension's longest-running partnerships is with a Boys and Girls Club in the county. For many years, the Fifth Dimension has operated in this club within a low-income neighborhood in San Diego, a good drive away from the University of California San Diego campus. The programming at the club, though, doesn't look like a typical Fifth Dimension. That's because the researchers made a conscious decision at the outset not to impose the typical design elements of the program on the site. Instead, they accommodated the site's needs and constraints. The researchers felt the limited facilities and the goals of the adults there were incompatible with the full model for a Fifth Dimension, but they wanted to form a partnership with the Boys and Girls Club there anyway. In the process, they learned a lot about a different way of partnering with the site, and the club proved successful in all sorts of measures of outcomes, from behavior to achievement. This success was in some ways surprising, given how different the site's design was from the Fifth Dimension design that past research had shown to be effective.[9] And—as is common in Fifth Dimension clubs—the undergraduates learned a lot about their own deficit views of children at the site, and they reported in field notes many direct experiences of the children's intelligence and competencies that contradicted those views.[10]

How did these outcomes emerge from the partnership, when the researchers gave up essential elements of their design? At first, the researchers and undergraduates from the university joined in the existing activities and helped the adult leader at the club with the activities she was doing with the children. They helped with homework and technical support. Undergraduates helped prepare a tea party organized for the girls that the leader hoped would teach them about table manners. Importantly, some of these activities—like initiating homework help—had never been part of the Fifth Dimension model, because they were explicitly teacher-directed rather than student-directed. In a typical Fifth Dimension site, an undergraduate might provide homework help, but only when a child asked for it. The leader of the club, though, had taken on responsibility for overseeing that children's homework was completed. The university researchers decided they needed to support the leader in this task, if they were to be truly helpful to her in meeting her club's mission.

Over time, some new activities emerged from discussions among the university researchers and students, the club leader, and the children. Some activities were useful because they served the distinct aims of the researchers and program leader, such as collecting and assembling report card data from students. This activity served the researchers' need for evaluative data, but it also served the program leader's aim of monitoring children's progress in school. Other activities were useful because they leveraged the outside expertise of university students to support emerging mutually held goals for children, such as improving the quality of the snacks they ate at the club. Some undergraduate students had gardening skills, and they helped rebuild the club's struggling garden, growing food that they helped the children prepare for snacks.

The university researchers also introduced some of the activities typical of other sites, and they facilitated colleagues' research at the site when it supported the larger aims of the club for academic enrichment. A colleague from a partner institution led physics activities with children using videoconferencing tools to connect them to student instructors in another state.[11] The partnership also helped facilitate a research project in which the children used film-editing software to make movies. Neither these activities nor the gardening project could have happened without the expertise and resources of the university partner. At the same time, these new goals for activities were ones that the researchers introduced into the setting; they did more than just add resources to support the existing goals of the club leader.

The researchers involved in this partnership describe this process of figuring out what to do together over time as one of *mutual appropriation.* The term points to the efforts partners make to change the initiatives introduced by the other partner and make them their own. Mutual appropriation is evident in how the Boys and Girls Club subverted some of the ways that university researchers sought to make programming more student centered. It is also evident in the ways that the university researchers sought to introduce more play-based activities into an academically focused afterschool program. Both partners "mangled" each other's efforts in ways that neither could have anticipated but that ultimately supported the development of a productive partnership and led to positive outcomes for the participants.[12]

The stance of attending to and even being willing to have one's educational innovation mangled by the other is unusual for researchers. Most researchers like well-defined interventions with interlocking components, each of which they view as essential for educators to implement with fidelity. For mature interventions, researchers may even have strong evidence that some elements must be implemented with fidelity to get good results.[13] But this stance is not conducive—at least at first—to building a strong, mutualistic partnership. It is far more productive to take the stance that the University of California researchers did with the Boys and Girls Club—that is, to embrace the mangling of their innovation and to see what they could learn from it. As they put it:

> [C]ontrary to the usual negative implications of such terms as "subvert" and "dismember," our experience, following our own version of a "mutual appropriation" approach, sees these features of the intervention process as perfectly normal and healthy. They are required for reciprocity, in which both sides of the interaction (organizationally speaking) are doing their best to achieve the common goals that anchor their continued interactions, while staying focused on their individual activities, which may or may not mesh perfectly with those of the other participants.[14]

Moreover, the researchers made the mangling an object of study; they decided to research how a system of activities like the Fifth Dimension could be pulled apart, rearranged, or even expelled from a site over time.[15]

A second aspect of the University of California researchers' stance is important to point out, because it created the necessary conditions for them to introduce new activities into the setting. That is, the university researchers began with the idea that they should first *be of service* to their partner organization. The researchers' activities supported their partner's goals—not their own—even when the work did not suit the researchers' own aims for being there. Though we would not expect an educational organization that is strapped for resources to do the same for researchers right away, researchers' entrance into a space is never only about service: their reward system involves doing research in educational settings that makes demands of participants. Showing a commitment not only up front but also in an ongoing way is essential for reciprocity in a partnership.

Being of service is an especially important stance for researchers to take in partnerships where there are long histories of inequities between researchers and community members. Megan Bang, an indigenous scholar in science education at the University of Washington, underscores the need for her team members to contribute volunteer time at the places where they conduct research. Researchers conducting fieldwork at a community center, for example, might pitch in to unload food being delivered or serve food at a luncheon for elders, if it is needed. Bang and her colleagues underscore the importance of being willing to do such work in helping to flip "the typical flow of work in research partnerships" and to be flexible about what problems are most pressing to solve at any given time. (See Tools and Templates, exhibit 13: "Whose Work Are We Doing?")

WHEN TO ADAPT THE FOCUS OF PARTNERSHIP WORK

Taking the stance that adapting to and serving partners' changing needs may be useful for building and sustaining partnerships, but it's not possible or wise for research partners to take on every potential endeavor. A small team must carefully consider what it can take on and do well, which includes considerations about both available time and expertise. Agreeing to help out but not following through because of limited time undermines rather than builds trust. And trying to help out with an initiative that goes well beyond the knowledge and skill of team members may lead to failures that could have been otherwise avoided and that sully the partnership's reputation within the broader educational organization. Teams need some good heuristics for when to say yes, and it is the joint responsibility of educators and researchers to decide what will make a good bet for the partnership.

One heuristic that the Inquiry Hub partnership uses is that anytime the team takes on a new line of work to adapt to a new district initiative, the initiative should be one that includes input and energy of a wide variety of teachers. In the team's view, there is no sense in adapting its work to accommodate a district-level initiative that is taking place only at a single school or that is peripheral to what goes on in the classroom. By contrast, if the district is presenting new policies or introducing initiatives that will affect the decisions made about what and how to teach—or what is sometimes called the "technical core" of schooling—then the team takes a serious look at how partnership work fits with and could directly support the upcoming shifts.[16]

A good example is some work the Inquiry Hub team decided to pursue in high school mathematics in Denver. The partnership had been working closely with a group of ten algebra teachers in the district to identify mathematics tasks they and their colleagues across the district could assign to students to supplement the district-adopted textbook. The Common Core State Standards in mathematics included topics for algebra that the textbook did not present to students, and district leaders were also concerned that many of the tasks presented in the textbooks did not match the rigor of the new standards. The co-design focused for two years on a process of identifying, rating, and developing supports for implementing tasks in classrooms, including classrooms with high percentages of emerging bilingual students (English language learners).[17] The tasks and ratings were posted—along with the whole curriculum—on a digital platform called the Curriculum Customization Service that the research team had developed and that was already available to math and science teachers across the district.[18] In the second year of the work, district leaders outside mathematics announced a major initiative to have teachers develop Student Learning Objectives (SLOs), a set of goals tied to standards that would be used in teacher evaluations. Teachers were to establish some goals for student development for the year, define benchmarks for progress toward those goals, and develop a body of evidence to support claims that they were meeting those benchmarks. The partnership decided to take a closer look at how it could adapt the work to support the process of developing SLOs.

Several considerations factored in the Inquiry Hub partnership's decision to adapt the focus of their work the way they did. For one, district curriculum leaders were investing a significant amount of time in the SLO initiative, partly in an effort to ensure that the development process would include a strong focus on subject-matter knowledge growth. It was easy for them to imagine teachers struggling to write objectives that adequately reflected the focus and rigor of the new standards. For their part, the researchers knew that the grant they had from the National Science Foundation required them to demonstrate the potential to reach a much larger scale than they had achieved so far. The plan had been to expand the work districtwide in the second year, but the team had decided to delay the scale-up to address teachers' concerns about the need for more task implementation supports. Integrating the effort with the SLO initiative seemed like a logical choice, because it would allow the team to piggyback on something the district was doing anyway. Looking around the country, the researchers noticed many other districts and states pursuing similar kinds of initiatives, so this kind of pivot might apply beyond the district.

The main question for the Inquiry Hub was how the partnership could pivot to integrate SLOs into the task identification and rating work it was already doing. The partnership could not have done so easily had two conditions not been serendipitously in place. First, the math curriculum coordinator and another colleague of Bill's at the University of Colorado Boulder, Derek Briggs, had a parallel project under way, working with elementary-grade teachers in mathematics to develop SLOs using a *learning trajectories* framework. Learning trajectories are testable, empirically supported hypotheses about how student understanding develops toward specific disciplinary goals for learning.[19] Several trajectories have been studied in elementary mathematics, and these informed the development of the Common Core State Standards in mathematics, so it made sense to district leaders to explore ways that teachers might use a trajectories-based approach to develop SLOs. A second important condition was that one of the students from Briggs's research project was already part of the Inquiry Hub partnership. Thus, it was feasible for the partners to consider how best to adapt the approach to fit the high school context, because they already had direct access to the process used for the elementary school project. A substantive challenge to overcome, however, was that the research base for building trajectories-based SLOs was much more limited in the domain of high school algebra.

The intellectual challenge of building a trajectories-based approach to designing SLOs, though, proved beside the point for the Inquiry Hub team, illustrating the uncertainty and contingencies entailed in changing course within a partnership. The implementation of the wider district initiative on SLOs stalled, and the central office underwent a period of great instability with both turnovers and a major reorganization. The leader of the SLO initiative left the district altogether, and the superintendent hit pause on its implementation midyear. When the Inquiry Hub team went to recruit teachers to participate, not surprisingly, few were willing to sign on. There was simply too much uncertainty as to whether the initiative would go forward. Ultimately, it did, but the difficulties in recruiting led the partnership to give up on this particular pivot in the work.

This experience suggests that riding the wave of a major initiative can have some potential downsides for a partnership. Riding a wave by shifting course can increase the relevance of the partnership's work to the educational system. But if the initiative itself runs into trouble, the partnership does, too. For the Inquiry Hub team, this effort represented a dead end. But fortunately, the team had multiple lines of work within the district and was able to shift its energy and resources from a grant to focus on one of those lines of work—developing new curriculum materials in science. This observation leads us to another heuristic that can be useful for partnerships: the importance of continuously envisioning multiple possible strategies for advancing the aims of the partnership. The "continuously" aspect of this heuristic is central, because environments of educational systems are always shifting, and some emerging priorities of districts *are* viable and even become necessary for a partnership to accommodate in order to succeed.

Sometimes a partnership needs to pivot in order to maintain the viability of an existing line of work by attending to how that work is influenced by the existing infrastructures of districts and how they are maintained. These infrastructures include some of the relatively stable elements of instructional guidance to teachers, such as external assessments. Many, but not all, teachers report that these elements strongly influence what they do in the classroom, and their judgment about the fit of an innovation to those elements affects whether and how that innovation is implemented.[20] Educational leaders in the partnership can't influence all of these elements of the existing infrastructure—for example, a district leader typically has little influence over the content of state accountability assessments. But they can influence some elements, such as district pacing guides and interim assessments. These are not typically the objects of design in projects led by researchers that aim to influence teachers' instruction, but it may be important to expand the work of a partnership focused on a curricular or instructional innovation to better align those elements with the aims of the innovation.

The efforts of the Inquiry Hub in science illustrate the usefulness of adapting and expanding partnership work—in this case, to support shifts in the district's end-of-course assessments. During the first year of designing a new curriculum unit in biology for ecosystems, researchers became aware that the district's secondary science coordinator was, in parallel, working to revise the district's end-of-course assessments in biology. The district leader was working with the assessment office to convene a group of teachers to revise these assessments on an annual basis. The researchers noticed that the assessments being designed were not consistent at all with the aims of the new curriculum effort. Specifically, the assessments did not reflect the new "three-dimensional" science proficiency aims of the Next Generation Science Standards—which integrated disciplinary core ideas, science and engineering practices, and crosscutting concepts—and instead focused on students' knowledge of isolated facts in science. Researchers worried that if the assessments failed to reflect the aims of the curriculum, teachers would not implement it, even though the assessments were low stakes. They decided to help the district write some extended tasks that were more rigorous and better aligned to the Next Generation Science Standards. The tasks underwent the same peer review as other tasks did and passed muster with other teachers developing assessments. They were included on the district assessments that year.

This effort not only helped build teachers' confidence for implementing the new curriculum, but it offered a side benefit of increasing teachers' proficiency in developing student assessments as well. It allowed the research team to use evidence from the district-administered assessment to look at the effects of the curriculum materials on student learning in the first year. The researchers worked with the assessment office to gather all students' data, from which they created a comparison group that was similar to the students in classrooms whose teachers were implementing the new materials. Then, they compared the assessment scores on the more advanced tasks with those of the students of the comparison group. Though the results were not as they had hoped—the scores of the two groups were similar—the effort was far less costly than it would have been had the research team needed to administer and score assessments themselves rather than rely on district-collected data.

The effort was threatened, though, when the leader in the secondary science coordinator position changed the next year. When assessments were revised that year, none of the three-dimensional assessment tasks developed were included on the district interim assessments. The team missed the deadline for writing district assessment items to be included on the tests, and had to administer its own assessments to both students whose teachers were implementing the curriculum and students whose teachers had volunteered to serve as a comparison group. Only in the third year of the project did the inclusion of extended tasks resume, this time with an even bigger effort from the Inquiry Hub partnership to help teachers learn to design three-dimensional science assessments. This effort drew on the team's growing skill and experience not only in developing these assessments but also in working with teachers at the national level to do so. Thus, this experience underscores the importance of continuously monitoring how stable infrastructures in districts are evolving, in order to stay abreast of processes like assessment design that recur and can influence—either positively or negatively—the work of the partnership.

DIRECTLY SUPPORTING IMPLEMENTATION OF INITIATIVES

As partnerships mature, sometimes multiple people directly support the implementation of new initiatives. In the Seattle-Renton partnership Dan is involved in (introduced in chapter 2), the researchers themselves play an important role in co-designing and co-leading professional development, for example. In another partnership in that district focused on a middle-school science curriculum, the researchers not only help lead the professional development, but also—along with the district's lead science coordinator—provide ongoing coaching to teachers on implementation. The same is true for the Inquiry Hub partnership: in that partnership, researchers take on responsibility for conducting regular check-ins with teachers on implementation difficulties and collect data that the partnership uses continuously to inform iterations on the curriculum materials.

These activities of supporting implementation are time-consuming and can easily overwhelm a partnership. Typically, both research teams and district curriculum offices are lean operations, not set up to be staff-intensive support organizations like the Success for All Foundation, which helps guide implementation of the Success for All program in hundreds of schools. No doubt, this is one reason why various consulting or intermediary organizations play an important role in the larger ecosystem of school improvement: they can directly support the implementation of innovations at a large scale. The problem is that many of these organizations translate research-based ideas into practice in ways that water those ideas down. Few have sufficient capacity to conduct research and guide continuous improvement, something that a research-practice partnership can—at least in principle—do.

There are some important strategies that a partnership can use to make the amount of work more manageable. First, plan out work ahead of time so that the people needed for the task of the partnership are available to help. Implementation support tends to be an "all hands on deck" effort, so devoting team members' time mainly to implementation support at critical times can increase the chance of a successful pilot or scale-up effort. Second, assign team members to specialized roles. We find it useful to have one team supporting data collection and gathering informal feedback from teachers in the field, while another team focuses on professional development and coaching. This is useful, because while research is essential to the effort, there is always something more that can be done to improve implementation. If the people supporting educators in the field are also responsible for research, the research can suffer. Third, expand the co-design effort to encompass aspects of the professional development. We regularly enlist teacher co-designers in helping the leaders of the partnership to both conceptualize and lead professional development. Teachers often have great insights into the potential challenges of implementation, because they have been involved in developing the innovation and trying it in their own classrooms.

Many of our teacher collaborators end up being the best advocates for innovations, especially when they have undergone significant shifts in their own teaching through the process of designing and testing an innovation. In a project Bill led to develop a suite of applications for handheld computers to support student assessment in science, two teachers played a critical role when it came to scaling up the use of the tools in the school district with which researchers were partnered.[21] The two teachers were a husband-and-wife team who taught different grades at the same elementary school. They had worked together with researchers on an application called Boomerang, which elicited student questions in science and allowed students to categorize those questions according to rubrics created by the teacher. Initially, the teachers were skeptical of the tool's potential, despite being on the design team. They thought their students couldn't ask good questions, and so it would not be worth the time to elicit them. But through testing the tool, they discovered capabilities for question posing they didn't know existed. When leading professional development with a larger group of teachers, they recounted their discovery, which was very convincing to others who might have shared their initial skepticism. In the end, Boomerang was widely used among the teachers who used it in the scale-up phase of the project.[22]

Leaders can also directly encourage and support teachers to spread innovations throughout their districts, as a strategy for supporting implementation. Dan took this approach as part of a recent initiative focused on curriculum adaptation in his district. He explicitly encouraged teachers to share the resources they developed in professional development with colleagues in their schools. The teachers were skeptical of this approach at first, because a culture established by a predecessor in Dan's role had led them to think they were required to implement district-adopted materials with fidelity, not share their adaptations with peers. Over time, and because the researchers decided to study teachers' sharing of materials with colleagues, curriculum adaptations did spread across teachers' networks, and those networks became increasingly more connected across the district as teachers began sharing with colleagues in different schools.

Partnerships can use technology as well to help support implementation. The Inquiry Hub partnership has relied on the Curriculum Customization Service as a portal for teachers to access up-to-date curriculum materials. The portal connects to a series of cloud-based documents that the partnership can continuously update without having to push out a new "version" for teachers to use in the field when something changes. In addition, the team has used videoconferencing tools to stay in touch with teachers on a weekly basis during the pilot implementation of new curriculum materials. The format of the weekly meetings provided teachers with opportunities to share what is going well and what is challenging about implementing the materials. It also provided a chance for co-design team members to offer advice and insight to new teachers on the reasons for particular design decisions that might initially seem puzzling. It took little time to organize the weekly meetings, and they provided direct support to implementing teachers while also generating a wealth of informal data that the partnership can use to iterate on the materials in real time.

As partnerships seek to serve more and more students and teachers and to work at more and more levels of a system, most find that they need to expand their own capacity to support implementation. When the innovations demand significant shifts to teaching practice and the system as a whole has relatively weak infrastructure for supporting teachers in making those shifts, the need for partnerships to build capacity is especially great.[23] The only alternatives are to narrow the focus of the innovation—that is, to make it less comprehensive in its scope—or to focus on implementing only in contexts where educators are capable of doing so fairly independently, without much support.[24] Most partnerships find both these decisions difficult to make, because more comprehensive innovations promise bigger transformations in teaching and learning, and educational systems must strive to ensure that all students have equitable access to innovations with the potential to improve student outcomes.

THE VALUE OF OTHER PARTNERSHIPS' IDEAS AND RESOURCES

One of the best ways for a partnership to extend its own capacity is to cultivate ties with other partnerships. The work to improve teaching and learning in any subject-matter domain requires knowledge and expertise that go well beyond what any single researcher or research team can bring, and such varied experiences with leading change that a single leader cannot be expected to possess them. The ideas, resources, and implementation experiences of other partnerships are therefore crucial resources for any partnership.

In many ways, though, the effort to "look outside" runs counter to norms in research. Researchers earn recognition in their fields for being the best in what they do, which is usually some highly specialized area. They do not earn recognition for being broad enough in their domain of expertise to support the needs of, say, an English language arts coordinator who serves emerging bilingual students in kindergarten through grade 12. They earn even less credit for adapting the ideas of other researchers in their own work, unless they can make some significant new contribution that extends or challenges those ideas. Yet sometimes serving a district well requires both depth and adaptation of others' ideas. For example, in Inquiry Hub's project working with Denver high schools, presented earlier in this chapter, the team found and adapted a process of task analysis that researchers at the University of Pittsburgh's Institute for Learning had developed and refined over many years; had the team invented one from scratch, the process would have taken too long and likely come up far short.[25] The team needed to be more nimble and humble than is typically expected of researchers—that is, quick to respond to emerging needs and ready to adapt a solution to the district's problem rather than invent one they could call their own.

Looking outside also runs counter to norms among educational leaders. So many educational systems are convinced that their students and political situations are unique, and that a solution tried in one place cannot possibly work in another. It can take inducements in the form of federal and state-level policies to try particular kinds of solutions—such as tying teacher pay to student test-score growth or requiring schools to purchase curricula that reflect certain principles about how best to teach, as happened under the Reading First program—for districts to pay close enough attention to what other districts are doing to learn from them.[26] And yet networks that link multiple districts and school improvement organizations together with research can and do allow leaders to learn from what faraway places are doing toward improvement. They can even learn from the differences that exist across them.

A good example comes from the Building a Teaching Effectiveness Network (BTEN), first introduced in chapter 3. This partnership was organized as a networked improvement community, according to principles outlined in a book by Anthony Bryk and colleagues, *Learning to Improve: How America's Schools Can Get Better at Getting Better.*[27] In a networked improvement community, a group of organizations comes together around a common problem of practice, and in the case of BTEN, that problem was new teacher retention. The network included the Carnegie Foundation for the Advancement of Teaching; the American Federation of Teachers; the Institute for Healthcare Improvement; two large, public, urban school districts; and a charter management organization. Designated BTEN teams from each school—which typically consisted of four to six school leaders, administrators, and coaches—led the BTEN work at each site, which Carnegie convened.

The work to improve retention focused on designing and implementing a high-quality, two-week feedback process for teachers that was based on existing evidence. The network initially focused on refining this process in a single school, but gradually expanded implementation to teachers in nearly twenty different schools. Importantly, though the schools focused on this common problem, they operated within very different political contexts and had different student compositions. The schools themselves were pursuing varied other reform strategies alongside the BTEN effort. In other words, the network was fairly typical in the diversity of concerns that educators brought to an effort where they were expected to learn from one another's implementation of a common initiative.

Even so, the group set out to achieve what in Carnegie's model is called *adaptive integration.*[28] Adaptive integration is actually an approach to achieving reliable effectiveness for an intervention across multiple organizational contexts. The aim in this case was not just to improve the average new teacher satisfaction and intent to return to the classroom the following year, but to shift the entire distribution toward better outcomes (that is, to reduce variability in outcomes). To do so actually requires both a diversity of contexts for testing *and* some initial variation in outcomes that can be analyzed to help diagnose why innovations get different results in different places. The knowledge developed from studying variation is intended not only to contribute to the research base but also to serve the improvement effort itself.

In BTEN, the network learned a lot about the conditions needed to implement feedback processes reliably and effectively. The network had to apply methods of improvement science—specifically, rapid Plan-Do-Study-Act (PDSA) cycles—with integrity, using data to analyze problems in reliability and to guide iterative refinement of feedback processes. At the same time, schools that just went through the motions of adopting a "compliance mentality" about the PDSA cycles didn't improve, either. In short, the team discovered that when people believed they could learn from standardizing the protocol and learning from how others did it, they achieved more reliable outcomes.

There is much that partnerships can learn from the BTEN example about the value of learning from and through differences in context. For now, we want to return to the idea that it is a certain *stance* that was critical to enabling mutual learning in this partnership. To us, the success of this effort depended on participants adopting the stance that educational practice is a collective, rather than individual, craft that can be improved through joint effort. This stance is counter to a view of educational practice as a matter of individual styles, where a professional's individual autonomy is to be respected above all else. The view of teaching as an individual craft is one that persists.[29] But it is challenged by evidence from networked improvement communities and by myriad studies that show the power of collegial interaction to support the improvement of practice.[30] We emphasize this point here, because in our experience, cultivating professional communities of practice that span levels of an educational system, and that include a mix of researchers and practices, is essential for mature partnerships to meet the incredible challenges they face when seeking to make big improvements to teaching and learning.

In the next chapter, we discuss another set of challenges that any partnership lasting more than a few years is likely to face: turnover and funding uncertainty. The three stances we have described in this chapter—that partners must be willing to "mangle" one another's intentions, that researchers should enter the partnership with the intention of serving the educational organization's needs first, and that there is much that partnerships can learn from one another—are key sources of resilience under these circumstances.

7

Sustaining Partnerships

Sustaining partnerships can be difficult work. Partners face nearly continuous challenges in their joint work and to the viability of the partnership itself. People change jobs. People leave for new positions in different organizations, sometimes far away. Organizations dramatically change their priorities, policies, and infrastructures all at once. The work needs to shift in a direction that one partner is unprepared to pursue. Funding for a line of work ends, and there's no new funding in the pipeline. Conflicts create divisions within the partnership that are difficult to overcome. These challenges are not specific to research-practice partnerships in education, but they occur regularly even in healthy partnerships, and addressing them in a way that stays true to the partnership's overall aims requires attending to the relationships among partners while figuring out how to navigate difficult situations.

In the face of such difficulties, some partnerships end, but others manage to survive. They are rarely the same after major changes, but examining the strategies used by partnerships that survive major turnover, shifts in funding, and internal conflicts can provide some useful clues about how to sustain partnerships. To be sure, analyzing these stories cannot answer the question of whether the partnerships were worth sustaining, given the specific challenges they faced and transformations they had to undergo. For any of us in partnerships, we have to make a judgment call as to whether the particular challenge facing us is something we can work through together, or something that requires us to go our separate ways and pursue other work that is more in line with our aims and values. (See Tools and Templates, exhibit 14: "Diagnosing the Health of Your Partnership in Difficult Times.")

In this chapter, we focus on four different strategies we've observed partnerships use to stay afloat over the long haul in continuously changing environments. One strategy some partnerships pursue is to *adjust course* when multiple organizational changes happen all at once. This involves shifting and sometimes narrowing the goals of the partnership to align either with the concerns and expertise of new participants or with new partners and organizational priorities. The second strategy is to *expand participation* in the partnership, either by bringing new people in or by moving people on the periphery of partnerships into the center. Expanding participation is a strategy for building a broad base of support for partnership activity that can withstand major changes in an organization. The third strategy is to *make the most of proposals for new work*. This strategy involves using proposal development to deepen and expand lines of partnership work, as well as repurposing proposals that were not funded for new lines of work. The fourth and final strategy we explore in this chapter pertains to addressing conflict: *check in and reflect with partners regularly*. This strategy involves routinely checking in to find out what is going on in partners' work worlds to help deepen relationships and sustain engagement in partnership activity over long periods of time.

ADJUST COURSE

When organizational priorities shift, people leave, and organizations change their structure all at once, a partnership cannot stand still. Partners need to learn about the new priorities and decide whether they align with the aims of the partnership. If the new priorities and existing aims do align, then partners need to figure out how to reframe their work to be relevant in the changed environment. And if the roles of individuals in the partnership change within their organizations, partners have to determine whether those people remain critical to the partnership work, and if so, how their responsibilities within the partnership might need to shift.

Even when new priorities align with a partnership's overall aims, most partnerships will need to shift course for the partnership to survive. This is a different strategy than was described in chapter 6 of aligning work to help a major new initiative, though in that case, a partnership could be said to be "adjusting course" to a new situation. Rather, this strategy entails a major reorganization of the work and focus of the partnership. A good example comes from the Middle School Mathematics and the Institutional Setting of Teaching (MIST) Project, an eight-year partnership between researchers and multiple large urban school districts focused on improving the quality of mathematics instruction districtwide. The MIST Project spanned multiple years and grants, including two large ones from the National Science Foundation. In the first phase, the researchers worked with partner districts to identify each district's own theory of action regarding instructional improvement, study the implementation of that theory of action, and provide feedback on implementation on an annual basis. In the second phase, drawing on what they learned from the first phase, the MIST researchers began to co-design learning opportunities with district leaders to support the districts' efforts to improve the quality of instruction in mathematics.

In one of the MIST Project's partner districts, the district leadership turned over almost completely over the course of three years in the middle of the partnership. Rather than focusing district improvement efforts on supporting implementation of the district's adopted mathematics curriculum through an instructional coaching model, the new leadership wanted the district to prioritize making sure all students did well on student achievement tests over more ambitious goals for student learning. In addition, they decided to leave all decisions about curriculum to teachers, and devoted central-office resources to assist schools in identifying and supporting students who needed extra help. The new leadership team also used central-office resources to create a new coaching position, not tied to any specific subject matter, to support school-based teacher teams by designing and providing professional development to them, helping them design and implement lessons and assessments, and helping them analyze student data to guide instructional decision making. The coaches were also to work collaboratively with both the principal and central office to ensure their activities aligned with the district's overall strategy for improvement.

At the time of these changes, the MIST team had been planning with district curriculum leaders to begin co-design activities intended to strengthen mathematics coaches' readiness to provide instructional leadership in mathematics. Both the district and researchers were concerned that what they had planned to do no longer made sense given the new focus of improvement efforts. In addition, the researchers felt the new district strategy did not recognize the central role of mathematics expertise in effective coaching; they worried that many teachers would not have access to a coach from whom they could learn, since there were not enough positions for each school to have its own mathematics coach. These concerns were not unfounded, since the researchers' own analyses of district data showed that instruction was improving, partly due to teachers' interactions with coaches who were more expert in mathematics instruction than they were.[1] The researchers expressed their concerns to the new leadership in the district. Privately, they wondered if this spelled the end of their partnership.

The district and research team decided to stick with one part of their plan: conducting research on the district's own theory of action for improving instruction. This line of work involved researchers interviewing key leaders in the district about their theory of action, and then interviewing principals, coaches, and teachers throughout the school year about the theory's implementation. At the conclusion of each year, the researchers facilitated a district feedback session where they presented and discussed the results. At the time of the big leadership shift, the MIST researchers had already completed four feedback sessions with the district. MIST researchers were able to continue this work, in part because some key district leaders argued both that it informed central-office decision making and that it ultimately aligned with the district's goals for improving achievement.

During the next year, some things unfolded as the researchers had feared, but opportunities also emerged. The math coaches that stayed in the district were assigned to schools but no longer had an easy way to communicate and collaborate with each other. In many schools, the people in the new coaching positions assigned to lead teacher teams in designing common assessments had little expertise in mathematics, reducing teachers' access to more expert colleagues. At the same time, the district hired a new leader for mathematics in grades 6–12, and his vision for mathematics instruction aligned closely with the researchers' vision. He saw in the researchers a potential ally for supporting improvements to mathematics instruction. Along with a colleague who had been involved in the partnership from the start, the math leader worked closely with the researchers to revise some of the partnership's original plans. They designed new professional development for the following school year that was no longer focused on curriculum implementation.

That fall, the team co-designed and then co-led a professional development series with the new mathematics leader for two different groups—principals and the new site-based coaches of teacher teams. With principals, the partnership focused on what it knew would be of greatest concern: strategies to help students do well on new Common Core assessments. These new assessments would require students to reason deeply about mathematics problems, not just solve them by applying memorized procedures. The professional development for principals emphasized that to prepare students for these assessments, teachers would need to expose students to a range of cognitively demanding tasks and get them engaged in more academically productive talks in class. With the coaches of teacher teams, the professional development supported the focus on assessment. But the work had a different emphasis from that of central-office leaders who had supported teacher teams the year before. In the new professional development series, the partnership leaders emphasized looking at examples of student work and analyzing student reasoning evident in their responses to cognitively demanding tasks.

The researchers were disappointed in the district's shift away from a focus on curriculum and the quality of teaching, because they questioned whether they could learn anything about instructional improvement at scale when they did not believe that the district's strategies would support it. Even so, they decided to adapt to the new situation and take advantage of a new ally in mathematics in the central office. They joined forces, too, with another partnership, to explore new lines of work related to the measurement of instruction, which would allow the partnership to continue after the second large NSF grant ended. The team eventually won an external grant to continue this work with the district.

In the moment, it's hard to know what the right call is when partners are in a situation like the one just described. Both the researchers and district leaders could have walked away from the partnership when the district reorganized and altered its strategy for improving student achievement. The researchers had to adapt in the face of these changes for the partnership to survive, and they needed some allies who shared their vision to make staying worthwhile. And for them to be allowed to stay, the advocacy of district central-office leaders was key. As in any long-term relationship, there was a lot of second-guessing of decisions made and wondering whether the partnership would survive. But at each critical decision point, the partners chose to keep working together for the time being.

The MIST strategy illustrates how a major shift in policy need not be a deadly blow to a partnership. What's needed is a way to maintain a low level of presence and investment, a perch from which to observe and learn about new priorities and people, and allies on the inside who still share the vision that the partners hold. It's important that the perch have some legitimacy—that is, authorization from organizational leaders to be present and engaged as changes are unfolding—for this strategy to work. In the case of the MIST partnership, the legitimacy derived from its decision to focus on a key external demand on the district that its leaders knew they needed to address: new assessments of the Common Core State Standards. From this perch sprang new roots and new branches for the partnership, and that is why adjusting course can be important for the long-term sustainability of a partnership like MIST.

EXPAND PARTICIPATION

One sustainability strategy partnerships can use is to ensure there is broad participation in its activities. Adding more educators from different central-office departments and schools ensures that, even if one person leaves or is removed from his or her position, other educators will still be available to serve as internal advocates for continuing the work with an external researcher. In a major reorganization, a partner representative may wind up in a new position that is equally or even more important to the viability of the partnership. Researchers involved in partnerships change positions as well, and so a team that comprises more than one lead researcher can prevent one researcher's move from ending the partnership. Adding students and postdoctoral scholars with interests that are related—but not identical—to those of the partnership's lead researchers can expand the partnership's capacity to respond to new and emerging priorities of educational organizations.

The broad participation of educators and the large research team in the MIST partnership partly explains its viability in the district that underwent major turnover in the central office. One central-office leader moved into a different position, where she supervised principals. She consulted members of the research team on the design of an initial professional development activity for principals focused on effective professional learning communities. It helped that the team already had leading researchers in the field on the subject of professional learning communities who could guide the district in supporting the school-based teacher teams at the center of its new district improvement strategy.

Expanding participation can do more than just help a partnership survive turnover; it can also help build the partnership's capacity. A good example comes from the Center for Learning Technologies in Urban Schools (LeTUS), a program funded by the National Science Foundation and organized as a set of partnerships among four different institutions, the University of Michigan, Detroit Public Schools, Northwestern University, and Chicago Public Schools. The main focus of the partnership was on developing curriculum materials in science that integrated new technologies to facilitate student inquiry. Different "work circles" comprising teachers, district leaders, and researchers co-developed the materials, and the teachers involved tested them in their classrooms. Many of the curriculum units initially developed by these work circles have been revised multiple times, are commercially available, and have even been tested in large-scale field trials.[2]

The partnership was a large undertaking for the team, and within a few years, the work circles had developed multiple units that the partnership could not support without additional people to help provide professional development. At first, in the partnership between the University of Michigan and Detroit Public Schools, researchers and district leaders co-designed and co-led much of the professional development in the new curriculum units.[3] Each unit's professional development required a weeklong summer workshop, as well as monthly Saturday meetings during the school year. As the work expanded to include more units and nearly one-fourth of the district's middle-school science teachers, there weren't enough leaders who could devote this much time to preparing teachers to implement the units.

In addition, district teachers felt as though the professional development led by researchers was not fully addressing their needs.

The team decided to shift leadership of professional development to a group of teacher leaders who had assisted with designing and piloting the units, moving them from more peripheral to more central positions in the partnership. The LeTUS team built support structures for the teacher leaders to strengthen their own content knowledge related to the units and to help them design the professional development sessions. They reviewed results from previous years' student assessments to help them decide what aspects of the science content should be addressed in the research.

As Laura D'Amico, a researcher who studied the partnership, reported, the shift had several benefits for the partnership. It helped the teacher leaders develop broader awareness of district initiatives, since district leaders co-planned the professional development with them. They could incorporate elements of these initiatives into their professional development, making the workshops more relevant for teachers. It also helped spread the LeTUS way of thinking about inquiry teaching by building a network of teachers in the district that were focused on improving science teaching. The members of that network shared strategies and turned to one another for help, and the professional development became integrated into the regular district calendar of activities—that is, part of the infrastructure.[4]

The LeTUS model is one that Bill and others have applied in their projects on multiple occasions. It begins with researchers working closely with a small cadre of teacher leaders, developing their capacity for design, and then preparing those teacher leaders to spread an innovation across their district. It is distinct from a "train the trainers" model in that the work is different for both the researchers and educators at each phase, but similar to that model in that it relies on developing participants as experts and leaders in facilitating scale-up.

MAKE THE MOST OF PROPOSALS

People in partnerships have to write lots of proposals for external grants to carry out design, implementation, and research activities, because there's no agency or foundation that will write a blank check for partnerships to do the work they want to do indefinitely. Funding for a research and development project typically lasts no more than three to five years, and most funders have an agenda—a specific set of priorities for research and development—that proposals must support. In addition, at most agencies and foundations, the number of people applying far exceeds the resources available, so the odds that any given proposal will be funded can be low. This funding situation not only creates uncertainty about the partnership's sustainability but also necessitates continuous proposal development. Most partnerships that last have had multiple external grants and developed even more proposals than they have had projects.

Compared to other arrangements, partnerships bring a lot to the table to make proposal development easier. At the federal level—as well as in many private foundations—both exploratory and design studies are expected to address practical problems of education and to justify the importance of the problem in proposals.[5] A partnership with a solid foundation already likely has evidence related to its focal problem of practice, as well as a sense of the stakeholders who care about the problem. Partnerships also often have a track record of success to highlight in proposals, as well as a clear sense of what more they need to do to continue that success. When a partnership proposes something ambitious and large in scale, a proven track record reassures agencies and peer review panels who might otherwise deem it too risky an investment. And a clear sense of gaps shows that researchers and educators are open to acknowledging and addressing what research might tell them are shortcomings of their strategies. Partnerships enable the rapid submission of proposals to meet opportunities with tight deadlines. In a partnership, the researcher already knows well the practitioner's priorities and system context, so can write a first draft to reflect those ideas, limiting the back-and-forth revision and negotiation with the practitioner to just fine-tuning. Likewise, the practitioner partner can secure the support and approval of school district leaders quickly by vouching for the researchers and framing the proposal as an extension of existing district work. Finally, an existing partnership brings a key set of resources and ways of working together that can boost reviewers' confidence in the success of the collaboration itself. This can help a partnership stand out in comparison to a proposal involving people who have never worked together before.

Still, proposal development carries significant risks for partnerships. Partnerships may be dependent entirely on external funding to keep their activities going. If there are no funded grants supporting their joint work, the partnership can dissolve. Also, when a proposal is not funded, people may lose confidence in the partnership or in the people who wrote the grant. They might decide that continuing to put their trust in an external partner to help write a grant is not a good investment of their time and energy.[6] It's therefore important to figure out how to organize proposal processes to share in the risk and to help advance partnership goals, whether or not a proposal is funded.

A story of a partnership in public health education between a university and community-based organization illustrates a successful strategy for inclusive and thoughtful proposal development.[7] Formed in the late 1990s, this partnership focused on community health and enhancing graduate medical student education. The partners' first federal grant was turned down for funding, but the partners continued to meet monthly and enhanced some of the organization's existing program offerings along the lines outlined in the unfunded proposal. The team was able to point to the enhancements it had made with no additional funding in subsequent proposals, making the partnership more attractive to funders. Ultimately, the partnership was able to secure funding for a number of the activities that it had hoped to carry out.

Leaders of the partnership attribute part of the strategy's success to the fact that they involved multiple members of the partnership in developing the grant. Nearly everyone in their small partnership was involved somehow in the effort, and they gave everyone the opportunity to review and sign off on the final proposal. As a result, people felt a strong sense of ownership over the planned activities and understood what their roles and responsibilities would be if the grant was funded. Participants' joint involvement also spread the risk: everyone would take some share of responsibility and feel the disappointment if the grant were not funded.

Research colleagues who have written unsuccessful proposals for partnerships say that the process was similarly beneficial for their partnership. It helped them to work with their partners to clarify their aims and think more deeply about what they wanted to do together. Writing a proposal also helped them realize some things they could go ahead and do together, with resources they already had. Although winning a grant is much preferred to losing one, when partners do the work of thinking together to prepare a grant, the time set aside for joint planning can yield good long-term results.

Making the most of proposals also means reusing parts of unsuccessful proposals that reflect what the partners most want to do, regardless of what a panel of reviewers has decided. When a new funding opportunity arises, there is no need to start from scratch on the proposal. In fact, it is critical to make use of the time that's already been invested to come up with a research agenda to develop the new proposal. Of course, it is hardly ever possible to simply submit an old grant proposal to a new funder "as is," because successful proposals always directly address the priorities of funding agencies. But if the funding opportunity is a good match for the partnership as a whole, then it's likely that some core pieces of work will align with the partnership's existing priorities. Given the ongoing need for partnerships to secure external funding, adapting those pieces to fit a new request for proposals is an important strategy for sustaining a partnership.

CHECK IN AND REFLECT WITH PARTNERS REGULARLY

As partnerships mature, conflicts and tensions may surface more often. Partly, it's because people are willing to share more of their underlying feelings about the partnership direction with people they know better. But conflict also arises from the fact that people and organizations are in continuous motion. Pausing on a regular basis—if only for a brief moment—to find out what's on participants' minds can help to sustain engagement and prevent some conflict. We all have things that from time to time keep us up at night, and in partnerships finding out what those things are helps us stay connected to each other as people and also helps ensure that the partnership maintains a focus on what is most important to participants.

Next, we review two ways you can apply this partnership-sustaining strategy: check-in routines and reflection routines. As we defined them in chapter 3, routines are repeated sequences of activity that people in organizations follow. By naming these activities "routines," we highlight how important it is to do them regularly. These are like rituals of renewal that we might undertake in a long-term personal relationship. We've highlighted examples that focus on advancing the work of a partnership, but these routines could also be social gatherings—a party or potluck, for example—that focus on renewing the relationships in a partnership.

Check-in Routines

In their partnership with the University of Washington and the Renton School District, Dan's team at Seattle Public Schools has a regular check-in routine that begins each leadership meeting. In this routine, people have a chance to share something going on in their work world that is significant to them. By encouraging people to share work issues beyond those related to the partnership's area of focus, the routine opens up people to the breadth of their colleagues' concerns, which helps them deepen their relationships with one another. It also serves a second function—namely, helping people stay regularly abreast of major developments in the university and school districts that could impact the partnership. Sometimes, the check-in routine leads into a more deliberate discussion of those developments, or yields a suggestion for a resource or contact in some line of work in which the partnership is not directly involved. On such occasions, the value of the partnership as a vehicle for connecting people to resources is enhanced. (See Tools and Templates, exhibit 15: "Check-in Routine for Partnership Meetings.")

In addition to bringing attention to institutional issues, these check-in routines prompt reflection on how well the partnership is tending to the needs of individual team members and to the partnership as a whole. Partnerships demand energy of participants, and that is refueled by personal satisfaction with some aspect of the work. If an individual's personal needs are not being met, his or her desire to keep up the work can quickly wane.

In design partnerships, where cycles of design and implementation unfold over multiple school years, both individuals' and groups' engagement levels ebb and flow. For leaders in a partnership, sometimes it is obvious why (e.g., it is the end of the school year, and teachers are burned out). But other times, it is hard to get a read on why people are being quiet in meetings or why conflict is arising more within a design team. A partnership can use regular surveys or interviews with participants to gain a better sense of what's going well, and what's not, at any given point in time. Setting up such surveys or interviews as a regular occurrence helps identify both reasons for disengagement as well as activities or events that are energizing and motivating to participants.

In a partnership to co-design assessment tools using then-new, low-cost handheld computers, Bill and colleagues followed a monthly protocol of interviewing all fifteen members of the design team—seven teachers and eight researchers organized into three different subteams. Each interview was brief, covering just four topics: what they understood to be their role on the design team, what decisions or progress had been made, what was going well, and what was not going well or was a concern. The interviews were invaluable in helping diagnose difficulties observed across the different subteams. As is common with multiple design teams, some move forward quickly, while others struggle even to get momentum. An analysis of these interviews revealed important tensions between the views on assessment held by researchers and teachers, as well as initial confusion about what it meant to be a teacher-designer.[8] Role confusion turned out to be the biggest source of difficulty at first for teachers, who struggled to engage with the participatory process being facilitated by researchers. Happily, teachers gained clarity and confidence in their roles over time, but breaking through the difficulties took strong intervention from facilitators to encourage their ideas and open a dialogue about the different views on assessment.[9]

Reflection Routines

In design-based research, researchers typically engage in many small cycles of designing, testing, and revising innovations.[10] The design process begins with the team defining the learning goals for an innovation, imagining how a particular set of instructional activities might support those goals, and anticipating how students might engage with the planned activities. As soon as a design study begins, teams almost immediately decide to adjust course on the basis of how learners participate in planned activities. Rarely, if ever, do students respond as designers anticipate, and some tools and activities always fall flat or fall short of helping students accomplish the learning goals set for the activity. After each session, teams engage in an "after-action review" to decide how to revise their plan for the next session.

A routine for reflection after a design session can be fairly simple. In the Inquiry Hub project, after each co-design session with teachers, a small team of researchers and district leaders reviews what people have written in a shared document that serves as a "parking lot" for issues they wanted to raise, and the team decides how and when to take up the issues in the next day's session. Then, the team discusses the plan for the next day and whether it needs to be revised in light of progress made that day. If any tasks took much longer than planned that day or entailed disagreement about direction, the team discusses these. Sometimes, the session includes reflection on the emerging learning needs of teachers in the process, as well as any asymmetries of participation noticed. Such sessions rarely take more than thirty or forty-five minutes, and they occur daily for the five-day workshops. Someone keeps notes in a running record of what was discussed, so that researchers can examine patterns that emerge from multiple after-action review sessions.

These kinds of sessions actually help to refine the team's ideas about how best to support participant learning, whether the participants are teachers or students. In Inquiry Hub's case, the after-action reviews have helped the team identify the rhythm of design and learning activities that a wide variety of teachers prefer and that makes for a good workshop experience. It has also given the team insight into ways to structure activities that recur multiple times within a cycle of design. For example, the design team regularly engages in analysis of student learning standards. The process is tedious and time-intensive, but it facilitates deeper sense making about the experiences that a curriculum needs to provide to students. Over time, the design team leadership has used reflection processes to revise the analysis activity into a "cooking show" version wherein some analyses are prepared ahead of time and some are unpacked or discussed more deeply.

The Inquiry Hub team also engages periodically in longer reflection sessions in order to make bigger changes to the design process. These sessions make use of feedback and data from student and teacher surveys, classroom observations, and professional development sessions. The longer sessions help the leadership team more fully understand how the co-design process can best balance the two different goals of producing high-quality curriculum materials and developing teachers' understanding of new standards and capacity to design standards-aligned materials. In these sessions, the team draws on a wider range of ideas to inform an initial set of conjectures—about project-based science learning, the role of relevance and interest in supporting student learning, and how engaging teachers in design provides insight into curricular purposes and structures, for example—as well as its analysis of data.

These sessions, in turn, inform more systematic retrospective analyses of both student learning and the design process. Of particular relevance to the central theme of this chapter—sustaining partnerships—are the retrospective analyses of the design process that researchers conduct. The researchers systematically analyze which concerns of teachers are taken up, as well as which ones are ignored. In some cases, these analyses prompt the team to make significant changes to the design process, such as ensuring that teachers are paired with a close colleague to whom they can turn when writing individual lessons. We will return to these retrospective analyses in greater detail in the next chapter, where we discuss how and what kind of data is gathered and analyzed in research-practice partnerships.

8

Research in Partnerships

People new to research-practice partnerships often ask us, “When do you find time for research?” The honest answer is that it’s challenging, because in a partnership, much of researchers’ efforts must go toward building and maintaining relationships. In partnerships where researchers engage in co-design, the problem is exacerbated; they are often focused on structuring design processes, maintaining a rigorous production schedule for innovations, and supporting implementation. All of these things take time away from designing and carrying out research, a core activity of any RPP.

In partnerships, researchers must draw on designs and methods recognized by a community of peers to get their results published, but they can’t apply those designs and methods in the way most of them learned in graduate school. If they did so, they would likely undercut the RPP aim of producing research that is relevant to practice. They would orient questions to theory but not to the persistent problems their partners face every day. They would collect data and produce analyses at a pace that is too slow to inform their partners’ ongoing work. And they would likely communicate results in ways that practitioners and researchers would not be able to apply in other settings. Researchers need a different approach to conducting research in RPPs, one that meets the demands of their partners as well as their own need to produce new insights and knowledge for educational researchers.

Researchers also need to find new ways to engage their educational leader partners in different aspects of the research. This includes seeking their help in formulating questions, in developing research instruments, and with some aspects of analyzing data. Educational partners also need to be involved in helping make sense of evidence from the partnership's activities. Researchers must devote additional time and assistance to create contexts in which educators can contribute their own insights from observations to consider alongside researchers' evidence. (See Tools and Templates, exhibit 16: "Reviewing Data Together.")

In this chapter, we describe what is distinctive about conducting research in partnerships, and we present examples of the kinds of research studies that can be conducted at different phases of the research and development process. We also describe forms of communication that facilitate uptake of ideas and findings from partnership research, both within the partnership and beyond. We believe that there are many "sweet spots" where problems of practice intersect with important gaps in knowledge. What is important is that researchers communicate regularly with practice partners what they are finding, explore creative ways to publish intermediate findings in peer-reviewed journals, and share findings in venues where there is a good chance that educators and researchers can take up the resulting ideas and findings.

There are important shifts for researchers to make, though, in order to apply research methods in a way that supports both a partnership's mutual aims and their own needs for producing analyses that other researchers will judge to be trustworthy and important. We highlight four in this chapter that we have observed are challenging for researchers to make, even after they've begun to develop a partnership with an educational organization:

- opening up different aspects of the research process to educational partners
- finding questions of mutual concern to educators and researchers in the partnership

- producing findings on multiple timescales and in multiple formats to accommodate the divergent needs of research and practice
- directly supporting the uptake of research by district leaders

OPENING UP THE RESEARCH PROCESS TO EDUCATIONAL PARTNERS

Partnership research is participatory; that is, those who are being studied also help shape the questions asked, data collected, and interpretations made. Of course, not all partnerships involve educators in every aspect of research, and it is uncommon for educators to share with researchers full responsibility for organizing and conducting research. But in most partnerships, educators play some role in multiple aspects of the research. In addition, the participatory nature of research in partnerships also shifts the role of the researcher to include facilitating deliberations about research questions, designs, and approaches to analysis—that is, someone who seeks the input and advice of a wide variety of stakeholders with varying levels of expertise in research.

The approach taken by the University of Chicago Consortium on School Research (CCSR) illustrates just how participatory research can be. In its studies, CCSR relies on a steering committee to structure educators' and community stakeholders' participation in research. Steering committee members help craft research questions, but they also can and do question research methods and researchers' conclusions, and they offer their own explanations for results that sometimes challenge researchers' interpretations of data.[1] Researchers facilitate these discussions and then afterward sift through conflicting advice and perspectives from different members in preparing reports and presentations to different groups. Though this amounts to lots of extra work—and different work from what typically happens in research and development projects—oftentimes researchers report "feeling energized because either they heard an interpretation they had not tested or they were pushed to take a research finding further."[2]

When educators participate in more aspects of the research, including helping shape interpretations and conclusions, it changes the meaning and process of "member checking" in research. In qualitative inquiry, member checking involves a researcher asking different respondents to react to his or her own provisional interpretations as a strategy for improving the credibility of the research findings.[3] It's something an individual researcher is likely to undertake in a variety of settings, over the course of research. Member checking in partnership research is a much richer experience and almost always is a collective process, characterized by high levels of investment in the outcome and argument; and, in some cases, other stakeholders' interpretation of a particular data pattern ultimately prevails. Member checking is about more than credibility, too. As Roderick and colleagues put it, it's about capacity building—that is, to build educators' "analytic capacity . . . to be able to address multiple research questions and bring data and analysis to the problems" at hand.[4] If researchers do all the heavy lifting of defining problems, interpreting data, and developing recommendations, educators' analytic capacity does not develop.

Opening up opportunities for participants to shape interpretations of research findings of course raises the question of how to manage bias in an RPP. The need to manage bias is especially strong in cases where participants have strong views, either pro or con, toward a particular policy or program. Bill's research colleague Ben Kirshner, who focuses on such issues in participatory research, describes facing the challenge of managing bias in a research study he conducted on school closures in a district.[5] He was partnered with a youth organization that was actively opposed to the district's school closure policy, and the youth were conducting research on their peers' responses to the school closures. The data the youth researchers collected yielded perspectives from respondents that were congruent with their own view: many students were struggling in new schools to which they'd been assigned because their own school had been closed. But more than half of respondents felt successful in their new schools, a finding that diverged from the youth researchers' own beliefs and experiences. The students played a significant role in managing the bias themselves, arguing to their peers that they needed to report this finding, because the research needed to be true to the experience of *all* displaced students. Only then would their research have credibility, they argued, in the eyes of district leaders whom they wanted to convince of the harmfulness of the school closure policy.

Most educator participants in partnership research share a concern about bias in studies, because part of what they value in having researchers study their programs and policies is an outsider's perspective. Moreover, educators generally value studies that are rigorous and balanced. In a recent nationwide study of school and district leaders conducted by Bill and colleagues as part of the National Center for Research in Policy and Practice (NCRPP), nearly all leaders (96 percent) agreed or strongly agreed with the statement "A well-designed study with strong findings can change minds."[6] This finding is consistent with earlier research by Weiss and Bucuvalas that involved government decision makers.[7] In that study, researchers found that the technical quality of a study contributed to whether decision makers judged a study to be useful, even though researchers believed that the technical quality mattered little to decision makers. This is good news for partnerships seeking to manage bias in participatory research; it means they can appeal to something that draws educators and youth partners to research in the first place—the desire for credible findings that arise from systematic efforts of a (relatively) unbiased investigation of multiple perspectives on an educational problem or solution.

This is not to say that managing bias is easy to do; it is not. Confirmation bias is a constant threat in human inquiry. The NCRPP study found that only a third of educational leaders said that research they encountered had changed the way they looked at a problem frequently or all the time. More commonly, the research leaders find useful gives them a common language for something they are already doing or believe to be true. Educational leaders are not unique in this regard, nor are they any different from researchers. Study after study shows that confirmation bias is something all decision makers must constantly guard against.[8]

FINDING QUESTIONS OF MUTUAL CONCERN

We often hear from researcher colleagues that the questions practitioners have about their work are "trivial" or not worth answering, because researchers have already answered them. The point of an RPP, though, is to address questions that are of *mutual* concern to researchers and practitioners, not just one side or the other. A question that narrowly focuses on the impact of a policy or program with a poorly defined theory of action is just as problematic as a question that focuses on some aspect of a theory of interest to a handful of researchers in a particular subfield of educational research.

In chapter 2, we explored some strategies for finding problems of mutual concern to researchers and educators in a partnership. Here, we highlight some candidate "question types" that can help partnerships go from an identified problem to a specific research question.

Our question types derive in part from early work by a committee of the National Research Council to develop a strategic education research program that would be relevant and useful to practice.[9] We find them to be a useful heuristic today, because they show different ways that research questions can emerge at the intersection of a problem of practice and a gap in knowledge or theory. Table 8.1 maps the five question types the original 1999 National Research Council report identified as key for the field to questions we find most relevant to defining a research agenda for partnerships today.[10] The examples named in the table are ones we discuss in this chapter.

Gaps in Knowledge

Although numerous studies and syntheses point to the potential of formative assessment for improving learning outcomes, interventions that actually result in improvements to student outcomes have proven difficult to develop.[11] Though many professional development programs have introduced tools to teachers that they could use to elicit and interpret student thinking, few have succeeded in helping teachers make use of assessment information to improve instruction.[12] Interest in formative assessment increased among district leaders across the United States in the late 1990s, after Black and Wiliam's synthesis of research on formative assessment appeared in *Phi Delta Kappan*, a periodical targeting school and district leaders.[13] One of the districts where there was strong interest in improving the quality of assessment was Denver Public Schools (DPS), and through a connection with a curriculum publisher, Bill linked up with the district to explore the research question "How can we best support teachers to adjust instruction on the basis of classroom assessment data?"

This particular question precisely captured a set of overlapping concerns of district leaders and Bill's research team from SRI International. DPS had just adopted a set of science curriculum materials, and district leaders wanted to focus on improving teachers' use of student assessment data to inform implementation. Bill had just concluded a study of the adopted

Table 8.1 Types of questions at the intersection of research and practice

Question type	Example question/study
Gaps in knowledge. Cases of problems that have been well documented (by practitioners, policy makers, or researchers) for which the existing knowledge base provides few workable solutions.	*How can we best support teachers to adjust instruction on the basis of classroom assessment data?* Study of a formative assessment intervention.
Unused and underused knowledge. Cases where there is authoritative professional consensus on research findings or best practices, but applications have not yet been developed or are not as widespread as they should be.	*How can we support teachers to implement cognitively demanding tasks in ways that support all students in doing mathematics?* Network to promote and improve the use of cognitively demanding tasks in math (QUASAR).
Incipient knowledge in the field. Cases where there is progress toward consensus on research findings or best practices, but further development and research are needed before applications can be confidently promoted.	*How can we apply findings about growth mind-set to improve motivation and persistence in academic tasks at the scale of a district?* Partnership to adapt brief psychological interventions in a district.
Productive conflicts in the field. Cases where the development of data, instruments, or theory would resolve conflicting claims and permit research and development to proceed.	*What mix of teacher design, adaptation, or implementation of curriculum materials is ideal for improving teaching and learning?* Partnership to test alternative models of professional development in science.
Dilemmas in measurement and predictive analytics. Cases where measures are needed to monitor implementation or provide tools to identify students needing additional support.	*What on-track indicators provide the most valid and useful data to educators seeking to increase high school graduation rates?* Research alliance's investigation of the validity and relative simplicity of alternative indicator systems.

curriculum materials, where he had documented improvements in teaching quality with the materials but not with assessment.[14] As other researchers had observed with other sets of curriculum materials, he'd seen teachers gathering data from carefully designed embedded assessments, but not using it effectively to inform their teaching.[15] The research project set out to design a new "workable solution" that would address a problem important to the district while also adding to the knowledge base.

Unused and Underused Knowledge

Beginning in the mid-1990s, a consensus among researchers emerged that the cognitive demand of instructional tasks assigned to students in mathematics played a key role in improving student performance.[16] The more challenging and complex the task to solve—that is, the more that it involved practical application of mathematics concepts and required students to choose what method to use to solve it—the better student performance was. The only problem was, this emerging consensus about tasks was based on systematic observational studies, not on intervention research focused on enhancing teachers' use of tasks.

In this context, a network called Quantitative Understanding Amplifying Student Achievement and Reasoning (QUASAR) emerged to tackle the question: "How can we support teachers to implement cognitively demanding tasks in ways that support students 'doing mathematics'?" QUASAR was a distributed partnership comprising researchers, middle-school teachers, and local professional development providers. It was less of a place-based partnership than something of a networked improvement community, in that participants shared a common aim—of iteratively designing tools for improving mathematics instruction—rather than a common context. Importantly, many of the researchers involved had led the observational studies that identified the importance of cognitively demanding tasks for students' mathematics learning.

The network was unusual, in that a set of tools developed initially for the observational studies was refined and transformed over a series of design studies into professional development tools for the improvement of practice. Two tools that were central to the effort were the QUASAR Cognitive Assessment Instrument (QCAI), an assessment composed of multiple open-ended mathematics tasks in several domains, and the Mathematical Tasks Framework, a framework for characterizing the cognitive demand of tasks as designed and implemented in teachers' classrooms. In QUASAR and subsequent studies these tools have proven useful in helping teachers to select tasks that support high-level student reasoning and to implement cognitively demanding tasks.[17] Other partnerships have taken up this knowledge as well, refining professional development models for task analysis and selection for the Common Core State Standards.[18]

Incipient (Emerging) Knowledge in the Field

In recent years, researchers have developed strong evidence of the potential of brief social psychological interventions that target students' feelings and thoughts about school for helping boost student achievement.[19] At the same time, when psychologists have taken these interventions from the lab into the field, they have found significant decreases in their efficacy that are associated with adaptations teachers make to them.[20] Driven by a belief that developing reliable interventions that work in a variety of schools necessitates a partnership approach, researchers from the Motivation Research Institute partnered with the Harrisonburg City Public Schools, Carnegie Foundation for the Advancement of Teaching, and the Raikes Foundation to design and test a new approach to applying findings from the lab interventions. These organizations came together because of a common interest in social psychological interventions' potential for improving achievement.

They adapted an intervention that had been developed by Carol Dweck's team at Stanford and was focused on building growth mind-set among students.[21] The intervention had been developed for older students, but the district saw a need for an intervention at the middle grades level. In addition, the original intervention was designed to last longer than the partnership was willing to support. The team made three adaptations to the intervention: developing material to make it engaging for middle schoolers with limited English proficiency, shortening the duration, and programming the materials to work on a tablet. Using these adaptations, they began testing and iteratively refining the intervention, borrowing a process used in improvement science in health care. The partnership is currently testing the intervention in a large-scale study throughout the district after a promising pilot study. In the scale-up study, the team is answering the question, "How can we apply findings about growth mind-set to improve motivation and persistence in academic tasks at the scale of a district?"

This particular partnership study makes a good example in part because there is broad excitement, among researchers and educators alike, about new insights into promoting students' motivation and persistence. At the same time, there's a mutual recognition among district leaders, teachers, and researchers that they do not know how to translate these findings into effective interventions that are usable across a range of school settings in a typical school district. Here, the team is conducting further research and development to demonstrate the feasibility of implementation and efficacy of interventions, prior to promoting its broad adoption.

Productive Conflicts in the Field

There are a number of areas in education research where there are conflicting claims about the best strategies for interventions. In the area of professional development, for example, there are debates about the relative value of online versus in-person learning opportunities.[22] Similarly, with respect to video cases, there is conflicting evidence regarding the value of viewing and discussing videotapes of one's own teaching versus that of a teacher who is a stranger.[23] In our view, these conflicts are productive—meaning that efforts to shed light on them through research could advance our understanding of how to improve teaching quality through professional development.

Yet another issue in professional development is the relative value of supporting teachers in designing versus adapting units of instruction for improving teaching and learning. Many researchers and district leaders argue for the importance of providing teachers with high-quality curriculum materials and preparing them to teach those materials with fidelity.[24] Others argue that providing teachers with the opportunity to design materials in a well-supported way actually builds their capacity to teach more effectively in the long run than just providing them with materials.[25]

This was an issue Bill and a team of district colleagues took up in a multiyear experimental study. The team asked, "What mix of teacher design, adaptation, or implementation of curriculum materials is ideal for improving teaching and learning?" To answer this question, the team compared teaching and learning outcomes of three different designs for professional development. In one, teachers were provided high-quality instructional materials in science with some evidence of efficacy. In a second, teachers were given professional development in how to design a unit in the same content area. The third was a hybrid design that incorporated elements of both. Teachers were randomly assigned to one of the three designs or to a comparison condition, where teachers could sign up for district-offered professional development as they wished. The study findings shed important light on trade-offs involved in the different designs for professional development: although professional development that provided teachers with materials yielded higher-quality lessons, students whose teachers got some experience with designing or adapting units learned more than students of teachers in the comparison group and students of teachers in the group asked to implement materials with fidelity.[26]

Dilemmas in Measurement and Predictive Analytics

Sometimes there is a strong convergence among educators and researchers on the need for new measurement of educational problems or processes. For example, two different sets of partnerships—one between the Strategic Education Research Partnership and San Francisco, and a second between the Middle School Mathematics and the Institutional Setting of Teaching (MIST) research team and one of its district partners—shared a desire to gather data on classroom discussions in mathematics. Over the course of a year and a half, they worked with a staff member at the Carnegie Foundation for the Advancement of Teaching to develop, test, and gather validity evidence related to brief student surveys of their experiences of mathematics classrooms. The district partners wanted to assess whether the district's initiative to promote richer discourse in mathematics classrooms was taking hold, and the two research partners wanted to know how students' self-reporting compared with what trained observers recorded.[27]

As another example, multiple partnerships have pursued research related to identifying students in ninth grade who are on track for graduation from high school, as well as identifying those who might need extra assistance to graduate. Strong interest in this area derives from the University of Chicago Consortium on School Research's success developing an indicator system for Chicago Public Schools that leaders have used to increase graduation rates.[28] What constitutes a good on-track indicator system depends in part on what data are available locally, as well as on the available research expertise in data analytics. In this vein, partnerships like the New York City Alliance for Public Schools have sought to adapt the work in Chicago, taking up the question, "What on-track indicators provide the most valid and useful data to educators seeking to increase high school graduation rates?"

Jim Kemple and colleagues at the New York Alliance compiled longitudinal data from multiple cohorts of students, and then compared the predictive accuracy of different kinds of indicator systems, including the one then used in New York City's schools.[29] Their analysis showed that while the system in use was good, there was a better, and fairly simple, one available that more accurately predicted who was on track to graduate and who might need more help. They also compared the accuracy of different subgroups of students and analyzed gaps in performance associated with race, gender, and socioeconomic status.

PRODUCING FINDINGS ON MULTIPLE TIMESCALES AND IN MULTIPLE FORMATS

Systematic social science research is a slow process, especially relative to the speed with which educational leaders are expected to make decisions. In addition, research always lags behind policy changes, and educational leaders often have to find solutions to supporting implementation of policies for which there are no "evidence-based programs" available. The best-case scenario often involves educators consulting with researchers to adapt ideas, tools, and practices tested in earlier studies to new situations. And they have to work together quickly—more quickly than social science can typically proceed—to develop and test solutions to new dilemmas of practice created by new policies.

Even once they agree on a course of action, it is difficult for researchers and educators to stay in synchrony. In partnership, researchers need ways to "speed up" data collection, analysis, and communication of findings. But they also need to make time to be "out of sync" with the speed of practice to explore connections between what they are doing locally with educator partners and what other researchers have done or are investigating in the problem of practice. Researchers need to take time as well to articulate justifications for their design, to analyze their data systematically, and to write for peers. The partnerships that are successful at this use multiple strategies to help them stay in and—periodically, as needed—step out of sync with the pace of practice. These strategies include:

- making the most of data archives to develop new insights for research and practice;
- using practical measurement to study variation in implementation;

- creating interim feedback reports to practice partners; and
- developing a pipeline of papers for publication linked to different phases of research.

Use Data Archives to Develop Insights for Research and Practice

One of the richest data archives comes from the University of Chicago Consortium on School Research. The CCSR archive includes multiple years of survey data from teachers, parents, and students about schools' organizational conditions, instruction, and students' experience of their schools and communities. The surveys evolve as district concerns change, and researchers replace some items to answer new questions. Researchers have conducted hundreds of analyses of data in the archive that appear in multiple technical reports, journal articles, and books that are read not only by administrators in Chicago but also by school leaders across the country.[30]

One thing that makes this archive so valuable to such a wide variety of people is that it has both been informed by a practical theory of school improvement and helped to develop and refine that theory. The founder of the CCSR, Anthony Bryk, led the development of the archive, drawing on his own knowledge of organizational change in schools. Over time, the analyses that CCSR researchers conducted of data in the archive helped refine that theory. In the book *Organizing Schools for Improvement: Lessons from Chicago*, Bryk and colleagues present evidence for several core supports that must be in place for schools to improve achievement.[31] Leaders in other districts have used this book to guide and monitor school reform efforts, even though these districts are far from Chicago. Part of the value, they say, is that it provides a common framework or language for their own improvement efforts that is evidence-based.[32]

In the Denver School-Based Restorative Justice Partnership (DSBRJ), which we described in chapter 4, researchers drew on administrative datasets to which they had access as Denver Public Schools partners in order to develop a more refined understanding of how the policies were being implemented differently across schools and with students of different backgrounds.[33] In their research, they showed that African American, Latino, and multiracial students were being punished more harshly than were white students for the same offenses. In addition, they documented the ways that schools varied in their implementation of discipline policies: those with a higher proportion of African American and Latino students were more likely to be implementing exclusionary discipline practices—that is, "excluding" students from school by suspending or expelling them. At the same time, the researchers showed that the alternative disciplinary practices being promoted in the district were having the desired effect among participating schools of reducing disciplinary disparities. They not only provided this analysis to the district in a timely technical report, they also published it in a leading social services journal.

Use Practical Measurement to Study Variation in Implementation

Data from practical measures, an approach used in improvement science described in chapter 2, can provide useful and rapid feedback to design teams on implementation that can also yield insights for other researchers. In the Inquiry Hub partnership, Bill and his team used practical measures to guide improvements to curriculum materials and professional development. The team's measures focused on students' responses to different lessons, specifically on whether they perceived the lesson as relevant to themselves and as connected to the engineering design challenge that anchored each unit. The measures also asked students to report on whether they felt excited or bored during the lesson.

The team collected over one thousand student surveys and then analyzed the data before it was time to revise each unit, with the intent of identifying lessons that were strongly and weakly connected to the overall challenge. The analyses proved useful for a different purpose, though—namely, for informing professional development. The team found that there was much greater variation associated with teachers than with individual lessons.[34] In addition, they found a strong association between students' feelings of excitement and students' ratings of lessons connected to the challenge. These findings suggested to the team the need for greater emphasis in professional development on the overarching design challenge. In the following year, the professional development leaders presented this evidence as a strategy to convince teachers new to the project of the challenge's importance for capturing student interest and enthusiasm.

The team also saw an opportunity in their findings to contribute to a learning sciences literature focused on student experience of project-based learning. Past studies of a smaller number of classrooms had emphasized the significant role of lesson type in students' experience of engagement.[35] With data from multiple classrooms, the Inquiry Hub team was able to discover a different potential pattern—one associated with differences in teaching rather than curriculum—that could be important for implementing project-based learning.

Create Interim Feedback Reports to Practice Partners

Researchers need to be able to report partnership study results in a format that is both accessible and useful to their education partners. Unfortunately, too many in academia have learned to write long and cumbersome sentences. Researchers also place a heavy emphasis on theory, sometimes burying findings that educators might find useful in their daily work. The peer review process, moreover, takes a long time. In some cases, it can be *years* between the completion of a study and the publication of findings in a peer-reviewed journal. By that time, the practitioner partners are likely no longer interested in the findings, and researchers cannot use them to inform their ongoing work.

Some teams have developed a practice of providing annual feedback to partners that summarize key findings. The MIST team, for example, created a fifteen- to twenty-page feedback report to its partner districts, detailing what they had learned from interviews and observations that year and providing leaders with specific recommendations for the coming year.[36] The team presented the report each year in an annual meeting of central-office leaders responsible for mathematics in the partnership district. The format for the report was new for the research team, none of whom had ever communicated research findings in a brief feedback report to a school district.[37] Over the years of the partnership, however, they refined the report and the process. Their partners, moreover, characterize it as one of the most valuable parts of the partnership.

Another approach to producing practitioner-friendly reports is to develop a report series. The SimCalc team, described in chapter 1, developed such a report series as a way to get analyses quickly to partners and colleagues.[38]

The team made a habit of creating these reports as soon as it was confident in the data analyses it had conducted. Light on theory and literature reviews, the reports were written in a style that was accessible to educational leaders, with brief executive summaries highlighting key findings. The team shared reports with partners and also posted them online. This strategy greatly reduced the time gap—an average of two to three years—between the completion of basic analyses and publication in a peer-reviewed journal.

Develop a Pipeline of Papers

Academics often tell young researchers to "always have multiple things in the pipeline," meaning they should have an article or book chapter in development, in review, under revision, and in press at all times. For most young scholars juggling new responsibilities for teaching, service, and starting a research program, developing a pipeline is not easy to do. In partnerships, it is made more difficult by the fact that there is so much up-front work in developing a partnership that it takes longer to "get things in the pipeline" for publication.

One way to address this challenge is to develop articles and book chapters for other researchers to read in each phase of the research and development cycle. In partnerships, problem definition and refinement is an integral part of the work. Researchers can develop articles related to this phase of work, especially when administrative datasets permit new insights for research. It is also possible to write about the collaborative design process, provided there is documentation of the kind we described in chapter 7 (for the project that developed handheld assessment software in science) and publish findings about it. Research on the design process can also contribute to theory development—that is, theories about how to design educational innovations or the role of design in building educators' and leaders' capacity. Early-stage design research can also be published, as well as research to develop validity evidence for measures. Researchers need not—nor can they—wait until an innovation is ready to be tested in the field to develop publications about it.

Developing such a pipeline requires knowledge of multiple fields of inquiry, though, the kind that specialists in a subdiscipline of education are most likely to have. To write about a particular educational problem convincingly for peers, a researcher needs to have a grasp of how others have studied the problem in the past. To write about design, for example, a researcher needs some knowledge of different theories and tools of design and of the design-based research approach. Likewise, a researcher needs an understanding of contemporary conceptualizations of validity to publish in a measurement journal.

The need for both broad and deep knowledge of current education research is just one of the many reasons that partnerships often require multidisciplinary teams. Assigning team members with expertise in a particular aspect of partnership work the task of leading publication development is important, because it increases the chances that peers will view the research as an original contribution. Distributing responsibility for developing publications is also eminently practical: it helps to make the work of writing in partnerships more manageable.

Of course, not all partnerships aim to produce publications for journals. Research alliances, whether district-based or supported by a Regional Educational Laboratory, often produce technical reports that are disseminated on the web. Few have time to develop those reports into publications with detailed theoretical frameworks and comparisons of their findings to prior research. But even these partnerships rely on a strategy of distributing responsibility for writing reports in ways that align with researchers' specialized interests and expertise.

SUPPORTING PARTNERS' USE OF IDEAS, TOOLS, AND FINDINGS

In a partnership, it is not enough for researchers to communicate findings to their educational partners. As Roderick and colleagues put it, part of researchers' work is to give sense to findings, build a bridge back to practice, and ensure that their educator partners understand and can apply concepts from research, further refine and adapt research-based tools they design together, and use findings from their analyses.[39] By the time a report is released, they argue, its key ideas should already be on the agendas of partner organizations. The report's release, moreover, should not be viewed by the researchers as "last word on a research topic; it must be thought of as the first word or the next word."[40]

The kinds of sessions that the CCSR and MIST teams lead with educator partners are one approach to supporting greater use of research findings.

Educators—like all of us—may need to encounter findings in different forms, and often multiple times, before they can see their application to practice. Researchers, for their part, may not have accurate intuitions about the implications for practice of a particular set of findings. Their recommendations may be off, and it is only through dialogue with their educator partners that appropriate interpretations and application can be worked out.

Findings are not the only product of RPPs, though, and different formats are needed for supporting the uptake of big ideas or concepts from research and helping spread research-based tools intended to improve practice. Design-based RPPs are well positioned to address these particular challenges, as the collaborative design process provides a different way for educators to "work through" big ideas from research and apply them in the context of their own work. Many partnerships also engage in direct support for implementation as described in chapter 6, helping develop the capacity of district and teacher leaders to make effective use of tools and practices developed or adapted in the partnership. Of course, implementation can be a focus of study, and results from implementation research can be used to enhance supports for more equitable implementation of innovations.

In recent years, there have been several studies of research use within RPPs, and still more are under way. Many of these studies focus on improving understanding of the conditions under which research can impact practice. But partnerships are fundamentally about the mutual influence of research and practice on one another. Studies of partnerships need to also focus on how the partnership impacts researchers—that is, the degree to which researchers' approaches shift as we have described in this chapter. And to support the conditions under which this mutual influence can best unfold, the research and development infrastructure must change so that funders incentivize researchers to engage in partnership work.

9

Building a Future for Partnerships

Today, many people are excited about research-practice partnerships, and rightly so. The partnerships we've described in this book have developed strategies that have improved low-income preschool students' literacy, expanded the vocabulary of middle-school students so they can better understand science texts, helped students master complex subject matter, and increased graduation rates by identifying students at risk of getting off-track early in their high school careers. These and other partnerships have helped researchers ask better questions to produce research that is more relevant to educators, helping to shed their institutions' reputations as ivory towers. And partnerships have provided educators with timely ideas and findings that they can use to improve their decision making, helping their systems become more evidence-based.

The future of funding looks bright in the short term for RPPs. There are a number of policy makers and funders today who understand that improving educational systems requires a long game, even if they cannot invest long-term in specific partnerships. The Institute of Education Sciences at the US Department of Education has strengthened its focus on partnerships and research alliances for the nation's Regional Education Laboratories over the next five years. This focus builds on lessons learned from recent investments in the laboratories' research alliances, as well as a field-initiated grant competition for researcher-practitioner partnerships. Private foundations, such as the Spencer Foundation and William T. Grant Foundation, are also investing in partnerships and the study of partnerships. And across a wide spectrum of educational stakeholders—from university deans to chief academic officers in school districts to big-city mayors—partnerships are becoming a focus of efforts to improve educational systems and revitalize research institutions.

The excitement, though, must be tempered by the challenges of building and maintaining partnerships that we have outlined in this book. Partnerships need to invest significant time cultivating relationships and dealing with turnover and rapid organizational change. In an era where we are asked to do more with less money, partnerships seem to need more time and resources than we as a society are willing to invest. Nor can partnerships design interventions or produce evidence quickly enough to meet the nearly insatiable demands of politicians and other stakeholders for immediate solutions to education's most persistent problems. In short, partnerships are not the magic bullet that we continually seek for education.

There are additional threats to partnerships that must be overcome to build political will and a strong national infrastructure for partnership development. The pull of one-way, research-to-practice models remains strong in federal policies that promote evidence-based practice. The increasing availability of personally identifiable student data is heightening concerns about privacy, which threatens partnerships' efforts to build data archives that can answer questions they want to ask. Too few educators and researchers are prepared for the work of partnerships—they need opportunities to cultivate the skills and dispositions required to build and maintain them. And our institutions are not likely to be able to change fast enough to meet the heightened expectations for partnerships among policy makers, funders, and other education stakeholders.

In this chapter, we outline a set of strategies for securing the future for partnerships—that is, one in which RPPs can play a more central role in improving educational outcomes. We are not the first to outline such strategies, and so draw on strategies that others have proposed and tested in the past. At the same time, we are also involved in preparing educators and researchers for this type of work and in efforts to help partnerships learn from each other. We describe these efforts here, and what we are learning from them, with the hope that others may join in a wider effort to build a community of partnerships that are working together for lasting, equitable improvements in education.

Policy makers and funding agencies are important audiences for this chapter. Whereas in other chapters, we speak primarily to people forming and maintaining partnerships, here we also speak to audiences who are in a position to provide better infrastructures for partnerships. We hope that people in partnerships might draw on the arguments presented here to advocate for a new way to organize research and development, one that provides greater incentives and supports for RPPs. (See Tools and Templates, exhibit 17: "Building Support for Research-Practice Partnerships.")

CHANGING THE RESEARCH AND DEVELOPMENT ENTERPRISE

At present, the research and development enterprise in the United States is organized around a research-to-practice model that rewards individual researchers for coming up with creative ideas for interventions. Moreover, the federal government awards relatively small sums of money for research and development in education, when compared to some other human services professions such as medicine, where there is greater political will to invest in research. The two major federal agencies that invest in education research—the National Science Foundation and Institute of Education Sciences at the US Department of Education—had budgets of roughly $1.5 billion in Fiscal Year 2014, a seemingly large figure until you compare it to the budget of the National Institutes of Health, where total investments in research and development were more than $30 billion. The education research and development system, moreover, produces interventions that are hardly ever comprehensive enough to solve problems with multiple root causes. And, unlike in medicine, there are few mechanisms or resources allocated specifically to support the spread and implementation of evidence-based innovations.[1] These conditions feed our never-ending search for low-cost solutions that oversimplify the problems we face in education.

Big improvements are possible only with a combination of sufficient human, social, and material resources on the one hand, and political will to take big risks on particular initiatives on the other. Over the long haul, it will be necessary to create more long-term, bigger-budget funding opportunities for researchers and educators to pursue together. No partnership can get off the ground and be ready for a major system-level undertaking in two years for $400,000, which is the current expectation and level of funding for the Institute of Education Sciences' Researcher-Practitioner Program. We will also need a long-term plan to transform institutions of higher education that prepare future researchers and educational leaders. And we will need new networks and infrastructures that link together partnerships across the country and offer robust professional education programs for people in partnerships. Building political will for these kinds of larger, longer-term initiatives focused on equity will take time, so here we focus on some strategies for changing the infrastructure that we think can work today to build more robust opportunities for partnerships.

The first change is that the research and development infrastructure needs to be tied to the practical needs of educators, parents, and community members seeking to improve outcomes for children and youth. Tying the system more closely to the needs of practice could make research more useful to educators.[2] One strategy for doing this is to increase the percentage of agency funding that supports practice-oriented or "use-inspired" research—that is, research oriented to solving educational problems.[3] Another strategy is for funding agencies to demand evidence in research proposals that the problems being addressed are ones that key stakeholders—including educators, parents, community members, and students—think are important and would be eager to help solve. Such evidence could come from multiple sources, such as a local needs assessment, focus groups, and letters of support from educational leaders that testify to their involvement in shaping the research proposal.

A second change that could benefit partnerships is to focus a set of research initiatives on some common problems or "grand challenges." Many large educational systems face similar problems, such as attracting and retaining teachers in schools that serve high concentrations of low-income students. Rural systems also face similar problems, such as ensuring that advanced courses are available to all students. These realities, coupled with the observation that many partnerships address similar kinds of problems—high school completion being one example we have highlighted in this book—suggest that a more strategic approach to funding research might benefit partnerships. This was the suggestion of the National Research Council report *Strategic Education Research Partnership*, published in 2003, which called for a more focused and coherent program of research and development that would move away from the model of individual-researcher-initiated research projects.[4] In our view, it is possible to blend field-initiated research with a more strategic approach to funding, such as through targeted requests for proposals related to a specific problem. But it is important that the focus of such requests for proposals be developed with significant input from educators, parents, and the community. Ideally, the voices of youth are included as well in helping identify priority problems. If the grand challenge arises solely from efforts to lobby politicians at the federal level to focus funding in a particular area and not also from local sources, then there will be insufficient collective will to solve the challenge.

Third, there should be some incentives for researchers in field-initiated research to work long-term with educational systems. One way to accomplish this aim would be to set aside some funds in existing grant programs for awards to partnerships that have a proven track record. This set-aside creates an incentive for researchers to maintain their involvement with specific sites of practice, which, as we highlighted in chapter 8, can help researchers stay closely attuned to the needs of practice. The percentage should be large enough to alter researchers' inclination to pursue partnership, but not so large as to disincentivize new partnerships from forming or prevent individual researchers from winning funding for transformative ideas for innovations in education.

A fourth change is to encourage more collaboratively funded grants in which both researchers and educators hold the purse strings (departing from the familiar model of awarding funding only to researchers even when they work closely with districts). Sharing funding can be an important strategy for overcoming fear and mistrust created by researchers using educational systems and communities simply as sites for data collection, without any sense of obligation to give back to those systems or communities.[5] Sharing funding is also one concrete way to promote shared governance in partnership, an important dimension of mutualism. At the same time, mechanisms need to be in place to ensure coordination, so that neither researchers nor educators use funds in ways that do not advance the jointly determined goals of the partnership. This will require in some cases more active grant oversight, even after an award has closed, on the part of funding agencies and foundations.

Finally, some research needs to focus on the explicit goal of building the knowledge necessary to make programs work in complex educational systems for all students.[6] At present, our research and development system focuses on developing evidence that shows a program or practice *can* work in a wide variety of places. But randomized controlled trials focused on identifying programs or practice that will work under "routine conditions" of educational systems will hardly ever yield transformative interventions, because such interventions often require altering those conditions. In medicine and public health, there are actually funding mechanisms in place and exemplary studies of the sort of experiments that can yield evidence related to the conditions that need to be in place to make programs work.[7] For example, researchers have used experiments to test the efficacy of different strategies for preparing public health workers to implement AIDS prevention programs and for disseminating information about effective medical treatments.[8] Funding for use of improvement science strategies—of the kind used by the community college partnership in chapter 2 and the Building a Teaching Effectiveness Network (BTEN) described in chapter 4, both facilitated by the Carnegie Foundation for the Advancement of Teaching—would advance this aim, since that research approach focuses sharply on promoting reliable and effective implementation of interventions in complex educational systems.[9] Moreover, such funding would be ideal for partnerships, because they have the requisite expertise—and often the authority—to make and test the efficacy of changes to systems.

STRATEGIES FOR PREPARING RESEARCHERS AND EDUCATORS FOR WORK IN PARTNERSHIPS

Partnerships require both researchers and educators to take on unfamiliar roles. The roles of researchers and educators can become blurred and can shift over time as the work evolves. Participants always feel as though they are crossing boundaries into the "territory of the other," but in a good partnership, it's all "other." No one is on familiar ground, and yet partners get a feel for the rhythms and challenges of the work over time, celebrating the highs and taking the lows in stride. But all of this takes time, and it would be great if people could get a direct sense of what it's like to be in a partnership before having to help lead one.

We need to help people cultivate certain dispositions in order to succeed in partnerships. That includes a willingness to have your ideas taken up and reshaped by someone who doesn't do the same kind of work as you or fully know your context. It also includes developing curiosity about and empathy for your partners and the worlds they must navigate. And it requires a kind of confidence that—even though there will be setbacks and difficulties outside your control—partnership work is well worth your time.

There are also skills and techniques to learn. These include collaboratively diagnosing educational problems and developing tools for engaging diverse teams in naming the causes of problems and identifying the beliefs, actions, and infrastructures that make them persist. Partners need skills related to facilitating participatory design, especially in design-based RPPs. A good partnership always has one or more people who can elicit and make use of diverse forms of expertise to come up with a novel solution. Partners need to become multilingual—to be able to speak in the language of research, practice, and even policy—so they can help overcome difficulties in communicating across boundaries. People also need skills in democratic, distributed leadership—that is, the practice of sharing power in leading large-scale organizational change efforts, making space for stakeholders with different and sometimes competing interests to inform and participate in those efforts, and building work environments where people's contributions matter and are held in mutual respect and regard.[10] This set of skills is not unique to RPPs: it's needed for effective innovation design and implementation in diverse teams across many sectors.[11]

Laying the groundwork for strong and successful partnerships will require multiple strategies. For education researchers, graduate education must broaden to include a focus on cultivating the dispositions and skills necessary to be a good partner to an educational organization. It means preparing researchers with a theoretical toolkit that can inform the search for solutions at different levels of a system (e.g., classroom, school, district central office) and across settings (e.g., home, school, community). For educational leaders, master's and doctoral programs need to focus on finding and qualifying research partners and using research and researchers effectively to inform improvement efforts. Such programs need also to prepare education leaders to cultivate a culture of evidence use and encourage leaders to look for research when confronted with a new problem.

Those already in the field need opportunities for professional learning to help prepare for partnership work. There are already conferences like the Carnegie Foundation's Annual Improvement Summit, where educators and researchers can go to present and learn from others using improvement science methods in partnerships. In addition, we co-lead, with several others, an annual summer workshop on Design-Based Implementation Research (DBIR), where participants learn about building and maintaining partnerships, collaborative design, and how to develop and use implementation evidence to make programs work effectively in a wider range of settings. Individuals seeking to learn about partnerships, as well as teams that represent existing partnerships, attend this workshop each year.

There also need to be more opportunities for people new to partnerships to learn by contributing to existing ones. This could take the form of multimonth internships of the kind that we have provided to advanced graduate students in the Research+Practice Collaboratory, an effort funded by the National Science Foundation to devise and test new strategies for connecting research and practice. In the Collaboratory internships, students have had the opportunity to contribute for a focused period of time to a specific project, attending partnership meetings to see how the project they are working on fits into the broader whole. In one internship, a student had a chance to field a survey of student interest that fed into a curricular co-design process for the Inquiry Hub partnership.[12] That student also attended the partnership's regular meetings with teachers and district leaders and participated in project research meetings.

For more senior people in the field, it may be valuable to support their spending a year or more with a colleague at a similar level. For example, an educational leader might decide to spend time with a research team that is engaged in partnership work in their local area or even one that is farther afield. Or a senior researcher might spend time at a colleague's institution as part of a sabbatical year, learning about leading partnerships, or spend time in a school district. The latter is something that some senior policy researchers have done to learn about a new area of practice and to cultivate new partnerships.[13] Researchers have also embedded themselves in school districts from time to time, as part of institutional efforts to expand districts' research capacity. These experiences are invaluable for helping researchers gain insight into the kinds of research questions that are most relevant to the day-to-day work of schools.

Some of these extended opportunities for people already in the field require significant extramural funding, and there are some grant makers who provide it. For example, the William T. Grant Foundation's Distinguished Fellows program provides funding for researchers, practitioners, and policy makers to become immersed in a setting different from their own. This immersion experience is intended to allow Distinguished Fellows an opportunity to experience directly the challenges faced by actors in these settings. The Foundation hopes that these experiences result in more relevant research and stronger connections among researchers, policy makers, and practitioners.

INCENTIVIZING RESEARCHERS AND EDUCATORS TO REDISTRIBUTE THEIR EFFORTS

A major obstacle to researchers who devote significant time to developing partnerships is their institutional disincentives for doing so. As many have pointed out, the incentive structures in universities privilege theory-driven over practice-based research, and tenure review committees have difficulty sorting out just how to attribute credit for collaborative research that involves more than one investigator.[14] This is a problem for partnerships, because research is problem-focused and often involves teams that have sizeable tasks for which responsibilities are shared. In research organizations outside universities, pressure is constant to "follow the money" wherever it might be available. This is also problematic for partnership research, because the needs of partners do not always match up with large funding opportunities.

A number of coordinated efforts are under way to change tenure and promotion policies in ways that could support university-based researchers doing partnership work. Many of these fall under the banner of efforts to protect a place in the university for "engaged scholarship"—that is, scholarship in which faculty seek to integrate teaching, research, and service in ways that are tied to their expertise but that also benefit their community and home institution. A regional conference of Campus Compact—a national coalition of colleges and universities, committed to the public purposes of higher education—has focused since 2010 on developing strategies universities can use to incentivize engaged scholarship in tenure and promotion review.[15] During this event, called the Faculty Reward Institute, teams of faculty members and university administrators can learn about these strategies and work together with mentors to revise their own tenure and promotion policies. These strategies can provide the support that researchers—including untenured professors—need to engage in partnership. There is an important benefit to these revisions, too, that should be emphasized: they help to expand scholarship on inequity, scholarship that is often problem-focused and undervalued in many institutions.[16]

The principles underlying this work are simple and straightforward, and there are a number of universities who have followed them to revise their tenure and promotion policies. First, institutions need to define what constitutes engaged scholarship and include RPPs in that definition in order to promote them. This book is one resource for developing such a definition. Second, institutions need to develop criteria for evaluating engaged scholarship; examples from some institutions include "richly conceptualized," "well justified and coherent," and "includes reflection on what has been learned."[17] Such qualities are desirable for any scholarship, to be sure, but these criteria represent a good start toward institutionalizing support for engaged scholarship. Third, institutions need to decide how best to document engaged research, which doesn't always appear in a journal article, but might appear as a curriculum that is adopted by a district, a new institutional process that improves the functioning of an educational organization, or a widely influential method for developing indicators of whether students are on track to graduate from high school. Fourth, institutions need to expand tenure review, inviting community partners, as well as faculty members with expertise in engaged scholarship, to evaluate tenure dossiers. Finally, institutions need to determine how they value work having a local impact in tenure and promotion cases. Where "generalizable knowledge" is prized in the academy, within engaged scholarship the coin of the realm is local impact. Effecting local change needs to be valued so that researchers are incentivized to focus their time and attention on things like supporting implementation of programs and policies in a school district.

Some independent research organizations have made strong moves to work in partnerships, despite institutional pressures to follow grant opportunities wherever they might lead. Some are doing so because they have decided that partnership work should be part of their core mission, and because partnership approaches will improve the quality of the research they do. But what has been especially helpful in enabling multiple organizations to devote more emphasis to partnerships has been the federal investment in RPPs. The government's involvement underscores the importance of incentivizing partnerships within field-initiated research grant programs.

At present, educators also have few incentives to focus on long-term partnerships, and in fact, there are some perverse incentives that instead reward "quick-fix" solutions to long-term problems. The pressure on educational leaders to get results fast—in the absence of any evidence that this is possible—is high. Under these circumstances, there is little incentive for a leader to invest in a partnership that requires deliberate steps to first build an infrastructure for working together and then embark on an ambitious design and implementation effort. Moreover, the speed with which issues and problems come to the fore and then recede to the background pushes against the need of partnerships to focus on a particular problem for a sustained period of time. Changing this incentive structure will require a change in the practices and culture of educational organizations.

BUILDING CULTURES OF EVIDENCE IN EDUCATIONAL ORGANIZATIONS

A challenge to making use of research in educational organizations is the fact that on a day-to-day basis, what is most important to teachers, principals, and other leaders is that there's a plan for the next day, week, or year that has some legitimacy with the people in the system, the school board, and parents. We say "legitimacy" knowing it is a political term. Over the long haul, certain initiatives to promote evidence-based policy and practice may steer educational systems to use research to maintain political legitimacy, but to date, few institutional structures and processes in educational systems place a premium on research evidence in decision making. While "data" are increasingly important and viewed as legitimate sources of influence on practice, they are often subject to significant "spin," and ideas from research about the best ways to teach and findings from impact studies are not ones that many educators are expected to consult regularly.[18]

Conversely, where there is a strong culture of research use, the use of ideas, tools, and findings from research is more common among school and district leaders. In a recent nationally representative study of research use among central-office leaders, Bill and colleagues at the National Center for Research in Policy and Practice (NCRPP) found a strong correlation between the leaders' levels of research use and their endorsements of statements about the culture in their department or district regarding evidence use.[19] These included statements like "Research is seen as a useful source of information," and "We are genuinely encouraged to use research as part of our ongoing work." More generally, an organization with a strong culture of evidence use is one where members value research as a resource for decision making, select strategies using evidence, remain open to change in light of evidence, and enact multiple social supports and norms promoting evidence use.[20]

A key commitment of systems with a strong culture of evidence is to conduct research and evaluation on their own initiatives. Many of the leaders who often use research in the NCRPP study also said that their districts regularly evaluate their own initiatives.[21] Districts with a culture of evidence sometimes also have a strong research and evaluation department, with a leader who has some level of authority within the district (e.g., is a member of the superintendent's cabinet). This is the case in San Francisco Unified School District, where for a number of years Bill's colleague Ritu Khanna has served as director of the research and evaluation office and close advisor to district superintendents in her district. Many districts have begun to embrace improvement science methods as one way to develop evidence related to their initiatives. In San Francisco, for example, Jim Ryan (whose statement opened this book) used practical measures to help monitor the quality of instruction in mathematics classrooms as the district implemented the Common Core State Standards. We are headed in a promising direction when educational systems themselves take on the task of leading and conducting continuous improvement research.

In places where there is a more robust culture of evidence use, research studies aren't necessarily studied in depth as in a graduate seminar, though sometimes groups of administrators read and discuss research together. Rather, research is used in a wide variety of ways and for different purposes.[22] Ideas from research are used to inspire the design of professional development, as a framework for leading district reform efforts, and as heuristics for monitoring the quality of instruction. For example, in one district we studied, leaders used Anthony Bryk and colleagues' framework for school improvement—developed through the University of Chicago Consortium on School Research—to guide their reform efforts. Researchers' names and lines of work are invoked, sometimes as justification for a course of action. Most leaders can name research that's had an influence on them. And they exert effort to acquire research whenever a new problem arises.

Developing these kinds of cultures takes time. Policies to promote research use can help, but those policies should not be so narrow as to exclude the many ways research is used in places where there is a strong culture of evidence use. Developing routines across different meetings of discussing research and using it in deliberation is important as well. Leaders who call a researcher when a new problem comes up can prompt others to follow suit.

In promoting greater engagement with the research community, it is critical that leaders call in researchers to help, not to "experiment" on children.[23] As Suzanne Donovan writes, parents would be rightly concerned if researchers jeopardized their children's education or limited their access to opportunities to learn in the name of experimental research. At the same time, school and district cultures need to make greater room for experimentation, placing greater trust in educators willing to take risks to improve their teaching by testing out new strategies designed by partnerships.[24]

BEYOND TODAY'S PARTNERSHIPS: IMAGINING POSSIBLE FUTURES

Partnerships today are limited by the kinds of institutional arrangements that separate research from practice, school from family and community. The possibilities for partnerships are greater if we push ourselves to think far more broadly about who can participate in them, the roles they can play, and the potential focus of their work.

Exploring New Roles and Possible Divisions of Labor

The ways that educators' and researchers' time is organized puts an upper limit on the possibilities for partnership arrangements. At present, a full-time teacher does not have a schedule that permits deep involvement in a partnership's design activity outside the summer months, afternoons, and weekends.[25] University researchers have to balance partnership commitments with service and teaching at their institutions. When something comes up, it is hard to drop everything to help an educational partner address a crisis, though partnership work occasionally requires just that.

Building the kinds of partnerships we need to improve education and that sustain us as partners requires imagining new and different divisions of labor for research and practice. One prototype of such a division is the organization of a networked improvement community, in which the roles of researchers and practitioners are blurred. Other possibilities are for educators and researchers to split their time between different institutions and receive compensation from each institution for the work they do there. Fellowships of the kind that the William T. Grant Foundation provides could make it possible for researchers and educators to work entirely in one another's institutions for an extended period of time. Such transformed divisions of labor turn partnership work from something that happens in the "in between" spaces and times of people's lives into the regular workweek. They normalize and legitimize the boundary spanning required to maintain partnerships.

Focusing on Creating Equitable Ecosystems of Learning Opportunities

Working toward equality of educational opportunity involves not just students' school experience but the whole learning ecosystem to which they are exposed. Partnerships are ideally positioned to undertake this cutting-edge work. In chapter 5, we described a partnership, the Chicago City of Learning initiative, which focuses on creating equitable opportunities for interest-related learning at the level of a large city. Collectively, the opportunities in the city form a kind of "learning ecosystem" made up of learners, their interactions with each other and adult mentors and teachers, the different settings where learning takes place, and the trajectories of movement across these different settings.[26] An ecosystem perspective recognizes that learning is not something that just happens in schools—it can take place everywhere, expanding possibilities for young people to discover new interests and pursue futures that schools alone cannot provide.

An ecosystem perspective also informs a new goal for promoting equity: providing all young people with a rich array of resources for learning in and across the multiple settings of their lives—in school, in community organizations, in neighborhoods, in families, and in online communities. To achieve this aim, partnerships will need to map the locations of these resources, explore how youth navigate those opportunities, and promote equity by addressing gaps in the learning ecosystems and by connecting youth more effectively to existing opportunities in the ecosystem. These are all activities that the Chicago City of Learning partnership is undertaking, but at present it is unusual as partnerships go. We need more partnerships focused on building resilient learning ecosystems characterized by an abundance of diverse, accessible opportunities for youth of all ages throughout the year.

Expanding the Types of Partners in Partnerships

Partnerships to develop resilient, equitable ecosystems of opportunity need different kinds of partners at the table. They need social service agencies, housing agencies, community-based organizations, and local businesses of the kind that make up the Synergies partnership, which is developing pathways for youth to explore STEM-related interests in a large neighborhood in Portland, Oregon.[27] Coalitions and advocacy organizations can also play a role in creating more equitable ecosystems, building a broad base of support for expanding opportunity for youth and putting pressure on existing institutions to better serve students from nondominant communities.[28]

Organizations well poised to distribute new content are also important to partnerships of the future. At present, curriculum publishers are rarely significant players in RPPs, and yet they play a central role within the larger enterprise of schooling in the United States. One model for how content distributors can play key roles in partnerships comes from public broadcasting media, which for years has partnered with both researchers and education providers to develop, distribute, and study the efficacy of educational media through television, the web, and classroom interventions. Partnerships in recent years have developed and tested a number of effective multimedia interventions that blend television, online, print, and face-to-face interaction in low-income preschool settings in literacy, mathematics, and science.[29] These partnerships show what is possible when organizations with expertise in content production and distribution—such as public media outlets—are central in partnerships.

THE NEED FOR A COMMUNITY OF PARTNERSHIPS

A fundamental reason why we wrote this book is that we believe that others can learn from how our own and other partnerships have organized themselves to identify and solve educational problems together. We recognize that research-practice partnerships often select very different kinds of problems to solve. We also recognize that different types of partnerships will be drawn to learning more from partnerships most similar to their own. However, our experience suggests to us that partnerships are quite willing to come together to share stories of their work, so that they can learn from one another. In 2014, we convened some thirteen partnerships as part of an effort to identify new tools and routines RPPs might use to organize their work.[30] The videos in a webinar series that Bill facilitated in late 2015 and early 2016, called the Research+Practice Forum, have been watched more than sixteen hundred times on YouTube.[31]

There is a growing need for a community of partnerships to learn from one another. Examples of efforts to build such a community include the network we've convened of design-based RPPs, as well as the newly formed National Network of Educational Research-Practice Partnerships (NNERPP) at the Kinder Institute at Rice University. A community can help new individuals and organizations find their way into partnership work, and can develop resources that help partnerships organize their work together to build on the ideas and principles we have presented in this book. Perhaps most importantly, a community can provide a supportive place where partners can celebrate the successes, savor the joys, and shed tears about their challenges and failures. Partnerships need a place to "talk shop" about the work they do, where they discuss how they go about their work rather than give presentations to educators describing their interventions or to researchers about their findings.[32]

A community can also develop accounts and articulate insights that go beyond what we have shared in this book, adding richness, nuance, and qualifications to the claims we've made here about how best to build and sustain a productive research-practice partnership. We hope you will join and be part of the growing network of people committed to this strategy for promoting dramatic, equitable improvements to educational opportunities in our nation's schools and communities.

Appendix

Tools and Templates

These tools and templates are designed to help partnerships engage in tasks we identified in the chapters of this book. We have used many of these tools in our own work. In some cases, the tools are new, reflecting our best thinking about how to go about the tasks described. You may wish to print individual tools and templates to use in meetings of your partnership.

Exhibits

EXHIBIT 1

Communicating the Importance of Partnerships for Implementation Research

Partnerships do not always address problems that, when fixed, make for good nightly news stories. One reason is that partnerships often focus on implementing initiatives, and most people and journalists think of implementation as something simple and straightforward, certainly not newsworthy.

A recent report of the FrameWorks Institute (http://www.frameworks institute.org/) called Just Do It: Communicating Implementation Science and Practice *notes that many people believe that implementation is a matter of just doing what works.*[1] *The following is a brief outline of an argument for countering that belief, by appealing to values of innovation and ingenuity that the Frameworks Institute argues can help the public appreciate the importance of tackling problems of implementation.*

Our outline focuses on adapting the argument to address why the work of partnerships in improving implementation is important for education. Your argument will need to be more specific, tailored to how your partnership is supporting implementation of a particular program or initiative.

Argument Outline for Partnerships

- Problems of implementation make many programs less effective than they could be.
- The complexity of educational systems leads to many problems of implementation.
- Partnerships engage, even embrace, complexity with innovative, evidence-based strategies.
- There's a need to apply ingenuity and innovation to problems of implementation, and partnerships can generate novel solutions to persistent problems.

- Partnerships develop new solutions, because they bring people together who don't normally think and work together but who have relevant expertise to solve big problems.
- In the past, partnerships have developed effective solutions to problems of implementation, resulting in big improvements to outcomes. That can happen here, too, if we invest in partnerships to solve our problems of implementation.

EXHIBIT 2

Deciding What Kind of Collaboration You Want and Need

A review of partnerships in informal science education described three different types of relationships that could exist between researchers and educators:[2]

- ***Cooperative.*** *One party provides a service to the other. These relationships are usually but not always short term, and do not count as "partnerships."*
- ***Collaborative.*** *There is a shared interest in a question or practice that researchers study, with periodic check-ins on a study's progress or results. These relationships and studies are not likely to be of a long duration; however, when successful, the partnerships may continue with new studies in similar or new areas of inquiry.*
- ***Jointly negotiated.*** *Researchers and educators jointly identify the questions to be asked, review data together, and collaboratively analyze and produce written or visual representations of the results. This work is both long-term (over years) and mutually beneficial.*

You can use the following typology as part of a discussion with a prospective collaborator to help you decide which relationship might be appropriate.

Types of Researcher-Educator Relationships

	Type of relationship		
	Cooperative	**Collaborative**	**Jointly negotiated**
Type of activity	Provide a service. Conduct an evaluation of a program. Conduct a researcher-initiated study.	Provide a service. Conduct an evaluation of a program. Conduct a researcher-initiated study.	Co-design and co-implement an innovation. Conduct a study of the innovation that addresses questions of concern to both partners.
Value of work to partners	One partner values more highly and has a greater stake in the outcomes than the other.	Both partners value the outcomes, but one partner has a greater stake in the success of the engagement.	Both partners value the outcomes and have shared risk in the success.
Direct involvement in the partner's work	Direct involvement is minimal.	Partners are directly involved in the beginning, during check-ins throughout, and at the end of engagements.	Direct involvement is evident throughout the engagements.
Requirements for activity	A specific scope of work is presented to the partner to agree to or not.	Aims are defined ahead of time, and outcomes are valued by both partners, but one partner designs and carries out much of the work.	The scope of work is broad, relatively open-ended, and jointly agreed upon.

EXHIBIT 3

Identifying and Recruiting Research Partners

Researchers are more accustomed than practitioners to initiating contact with potential partners. Armed with their familiarity of grant funding streams and how to package proposals, researchers with an idea for a project can identify a pool of practitioners through easily gathered criteria—size, demographics, locality, or publicly known initiatives of school districts, for example. Practitioners, on the other hand, lack comparable access to the research community to scan for potential partners, and they typically do not have experience enticing researchers to invest time and effort in the work of a school district that may be unfamiliar. However, practitioners can solicit researchers to initiate a relationship that may ultimately evolve into a partnership. Practitioners can use the following strategies, organized in stages, as a tool to identify and recruit potential research partners.

Strategies for Recruiting a Research Partner

Stage 1: Prepare for a Research Partner

Identify the different ways you can characterize your initiatives or problems of practice that might be novel or interesting to a researcher. Identify what you want to learn through the development and implementation of your initiatives, and what intellectual or other resources you seek for support.

Stage 2: Pool Potential Research Partners

Draft a list of people with expertise that could be valuable in a partnership focused on your work. Consider people you value and learn from, through articles and other media. Search journal articles and books for authors with relevant expertise. Ask friends or colleagues you trust to point you toward people with relevant expertise whom they can vouch for as productive and respectful partners.

Stage 3: Pilot Resources and Tools from Potential Research Partners

In the context of your work, try out resources—tools, conceptual frames, or other products—that have been developed by researchers you've identified as potential partners. This familiarizes you with what they might have to offer and enables you to speak in an informed way about their interests when you contact them. As you use their resources, gather something that might be valuable to them, such as feedback, revised versions of their resources to improve their use, or data about how the resources were used in your setting. This demonstrates to potential partners that you have something to offer them, making their investment of time and attention worthwhile.

Stage 4: Pitch Potential Research Partners

Use your contacts and networks to broker an introduction with researchers of interest or "cold call" the researcher with an e-mail. Use a simple template like the following to make multiple contacts efficient:

- I am [your title and district], and I want to thank you for your valuable work in [insert field or topic]. We have used your resources to . . .
- [Describe more detail about your setting with a goal of communicating scope and scale of your work.]
- "Please let me know if there are ways I can go about the work in my district that would help you continue your work. For example, we could provide you with more information about how your resources are influencing our district's work or possibly collect particular types of data of interest to you."
- Request a phone call, and thank them again.

EXHIBIT 4

Initiating a Partnership Meeting

Partnerships can be explored even when individuals do not share a history and when a specific project does not present itself. Through contacts in your professional network, you can identify potential partners based on their disposition for partnership and their degree of authority within their institutions. Invitations for exploratory meetings should be framed to be enticing in some way and to establish the generative nature of a meeting, rather than the more common setup of a pitch for a project made by one individual to others.

The following is an e-mail a school district science manager used to recruit potential partners to an exploratory meeting. A respected and influential regional science education service provider gained commitments from school district superintendents to convene their leadership teams at an event for facilitated planning of transitions to the Next Generation Science Standards (NGSS). The various districts' science curriculum leaders valued this opportunity to garner support for science education initiatives internally, but the science manager leveraged the event to explore external partnerships. Because the science manager had no experience working with the people he invited, he relied on a trusted colleague to identify the right people and to broker introductions, which foregrounded his invitational e-mail.

Use the study questions at the end to consider how you could recruit potential partners to a similar exploratory meeting.

Sample E-Mail Invitation

To: City Department of Education and Early Learning School Partnerships Manager and Summer Programs Manager, City Public Library Digital Learning Manager and Community Partnerships Director, School District Community Partnerships Director
From: School district science manager
Subject: Next Generation Science Standards (NGSS) event at Education Center

Hi everyone,
You may have heard about the event hosted by the Education Center, described in the attached flyer, and X mentioned that I'd be contacting you in her e-mail introducing us last week. I'd like to invite you to join me if you're interested.

Rather than assemble my regular science curriculum & instruction team for this event, I'd like to think outside the typical district box and engage with community partners like you to identify how we might coordinate our work for youth with respect to NGSS. I'll also admit, as I said to X, that I'm interested in forming a team for the event that would be stimulating to work with for the day—X said you fit that bill! My hopes for our team discussions:

- For us to have common understanding of how NGSS is different from previous science standards and why NGSS is important for our youth
- For you to learn the school district's vision, plans, and current activities supporting NGSS transitions
- For me to learn your ideas, plans, activities—or questions—for supporting youth in engaging with NGSS
- For us to jointly identify how we might coordinate our work supporting youth in science and engineering

Let me know if you're interested in joining me. I'm really looking forward to learning from each other and exploring opportunities to support each other's work for youth!

Thanks,
[School district science manager]

Study Questions

- The invitees were recommended by a colleague based on their scope of authority in their institutions and disposition to partnerships. What dispositions in partners are important to you? Which of your colleagues or contacts are good brokers for initiating contacts with potential partners?
- What might the recipients of the e-mail find enticing about the meeting, and how does the invitation convey this? What would be interesting and enticing to people you would contact for potential partnership?
- How would you describe the tone set for the meeting? What tone would you want to set, and how would you do that in an invitation?
- In what ways would you want an exploratory meeting to differ from typical meetings with external institutions in your context, and how would you frame your different intentions in an invitation?
- How would you prepare your team to productively engage in an exploratory meeting, after an invitation is successful?

EXHIBIT 5

Conducting Introductory Meetings with Potential Partners

Often the origin of a partnership is a specific project, proposed by one institution to another, with deeper partnership evolving over time. Alternatively, foundations for a partnership can be laid without a specific project in mind. Potential partners can explore one another's interests, expertise, values, and general sense of what it would be like to work together. After familiarity and trust have been established, partners can jointly develop a proposal for work when an opportunity presents itself.

The following is an example of an agenda for a meeting that occurred between an urban school district, the city's housing authority department, and STEM education researchers from the local university, to explore ways they might work together to improve equitable STEM education for the city's youth. The school district science manager had a history with each of the people present, but the others had not met. He knew they had overlapping values and interests, complementary expertise, and the potential to work together in a fulfilling partnership. Use this as a template to pattern an agenda for an exploratory meeting between potential partners in your context. To aid your use of this agenda as a tool, the righthand column is an annotation with questions participants should consider.

Sample Agenda

Topic: Introductory discussion of potential STEM-focused partnership

Attendees: City School District, City Housing Authority, State University STEM education researchers

Intended outcomes:

- Knowledge of each other's work
- Identification of potential jointly pursued activity
- Next steps to move forward on activity
- How to name or label the activity for 2–3 audiences or stakeholders

Agenda items	Questions participants consider as they listen
[10 min] Introductions and overview of agenda	How is this exploratory meeting different from a typical proposal pitch meeting?
[15 min] City school district science manager • Strategic plan initiatives • District organizational and authority structures • Assessment context • Current science professional development initiatives • Challenges, problems of practice, opportunities • Clarification and discussion	Can I connect my interests to the district's overall strategic plans? What is the scope of authority of the science manager? What is a partial "map of the system" to consider leverage points? How can I connect my work to the various high-stakes and low-stakes assessments in the district? What dimensions of the science manager's work connect to my work and interests?
[15 min] City school district community partnership director • Director's role and department vision • Previous and current partnership work • Current capabilities and capacities • Challenges, problems of practice, opportunities • Clarification and discussion	What is the scope of authority of the community partnership director? Am I confident that this person knows how to partner with others effectively and respectfully? What is the scale of possibility for partnering? What dimensions of the community partnership director's work connect to my work and interests?

<table>
<tr><th>Agenda items</th><th>Questions participants consider as they listen</th></tr>
<tr><td>[15 min] City housing authority strategy director<ul><li>Director's role and relationship with city school district</li><li>Previous and current partnership work</li><li>Current capabilities and capacities</li><li>Challenges, problems of practice, opportunities</li><li>Clarification and discussion</li></ul></td><td>What is the scope of authority of the housing authority strategy director? Am I confident that this person knows how to partner with others effectively and respectfully? What is the scale of possibility for partnering? What dimensions of the housing authority strategy director's work connect to my work and interests?</td></tr>
<tr><td>[15 min] State university STEM education researchers<ul><li>Expertise and interests</li><li>Previous and current partnership work</li><li>Current capabilities and capacities</li><li>Challenges, problems of practice, opportunities</li><li>Clarification and discussion</li></ul></td><td>What interests and values do I share in common with the researchers? What expertise do they have that complements my own, and vice versa? Am I confident that they know how to partner with others effectively and respectfully? What is the scale of possibility for partnering? What dimensions of the researchers' work connect to my work and interests?</td></tr>
<tr><td>[20 min] Discussion of potential jointly pursued activity<ul><li>What do you need for a partnership to work for you, and what limits do you have?</li><li>What interests you most in someone else's work?</li></ul></td><td>What conditions need to be met by the potential partners—institutionally and personally? What activities could be pursued jointly with little investment, prior to committing to a full partnership?</td></tr>
<tr><td>[10 min] Next steps</td><td>What small actions could we each take? Should we meet again?</td></tr>
<tr><td>[10 min] How to name or label our activity for 2–3 audiences or stakeholders</td><td>How would each of the participants respond to others in their organization when asked, "What was that meeting on your calendar about?" How are the participants framing the conversation for their own organizational audiences, and to whom do they need to answer in their organization? How can I adopt some of their framing? What common language is the group developing?</td></tr>
</table>

EXHIBIT 6

Developing Empathy for Partners

This activity is intended to help develop empathy for different perspectives on a problem of practice that a partnership is addressing. It is likely to work best when there is already a focus for joint work, but when people are likely to have very different conceptions of the challenges that the partnership will face in addressing the problem of practice. These differing conceptions can arise from the fact that people occupy different roles within the same organization or because they work in different types of organizations. They can also arise from differences in individuals' values, identities, and histories. Whatever the source, this activity pushes each person to become explicit about their own conceptions of the problem to be solved and to describe the problem from different points of view.

Empathy-Building Activity

Part 1: Discussion in Role-Alike Groups (15–20 minutes)

Form groups that are composed of people with similar roles in their organization or in the partnerships. If there are power or status differences within an organization, it may be useful to create groups of people who are peers in that organization. Groups should be no larger than four people. Name the groups A, B, C, D, and so on.

In role-alike groups, participants develop answers to the questions:

- What do we see as the biggest challenges to overcome, to meet the goals we have set for the partnership right now? (Be sure to replace the last part of the question with specific language about the goals, such as "to meet our goal of increasing the high school graduation rate by 15%.")
- What do you think [Group B, C, D, E] sees as the biggest challenges to overcome?

Part 2: Discussion in Mixed Groups (20 minutes)

Next, form groups composed of one member of each of the different groups. Share out what that group discussed. When sharing what he or she imagines other groups' views to be, the person sharing should invite a member of that group to correct or help refine his or her understanding of the problem.

Part 3: Whole-Group Discussion (20 minutes)

Begin the whole-group discussion by asking participants to share what they learned about other groups' perceptions of the problem from the mixed-group discussion. Next, the facilitator leads a discussion of what commonalities and differences in problem conceptions they heard. If desired, build some elements together of a shared description of the key challenges the group needs to address.

EXHIBIT 7

Are We a Partnership Yet?

When you first begin to collaborate with a university or educational organization, your collaboration is not yet a partnership. There are some markers, though, that you can use to help you diagnose where you are on the path to becoming a partnership. The following table is a diagnostic rubric based on a framework for assessing the development and impacts of research-practice partnerships developed by Erin Henrick, Paul Cobb, Kara Jackson, Tiffany Clark, and Bill Penuel with funding from the William T. Grant Foundation.

You can use this rubric as the basis for a discussion with your partners about your partnership's development. You could begin by asking individuals to write down where they think the partnership is along each of the dimensions of the framework. Then, ask individuals to share their ideas and reasons for locating the partnership where they did. In the whole-group discussion, encourage everyone to listen carefully to one another. Expect that different participants will have different views on where the partnership is in its development. Not everyone needs to have the same viewpoint, either, for the participants to learn from this discussion.

Diagnostic Rubric

Dimension	Early phase	Middle phase	Maturing
		Process dimensions	
Cultivate partnership relationships	We have an intention to learn from one another and expectation that partners bring relevant expertise to solving problems. We have a willingness to try on new and different roles from what is typical of researchers and educators. We are curious about how we can help each other.	We are clarifying new roles within partnerships where authority is shared among educators and researchers. We are developing a sense of where we can best help each other.	We have a strong identity as a partnership and an open-ended commitment to ongoing partnership.
Develop capacity to engage in partnership work	We have human, social, and material resources needed to work in the short term on a specific engagement. We are seeking funding or have a first project that is newly funded.	We have human, social, and material resources needed to work a single line of work involving more than one project. We have two or more projects' current funding.	We have human, social, and material resources needed to engage in multiple lines of work that evolve. We have sought and won funding together multiple times.
		Impact dimensions	
Impact local improvement efforts	We are identifying a specific strategy for improvement and developing ways of evaluating the strategy, once the problem is specified.	We are improving organizational policies and processes that directly impact classrooms. We are making use of evidence and professional judgment about progress toward our aims.	We are impacting classroom outcomes. We are using our professional judgment and evidence about variation to improve reliability of implementation and outcomes.

continued

Dimension	Early phase	Middle phase	Maturing
Conduct and use rigorous and relevant research	We are developing evidence of the nature and relevance of the focal problem of practice to different stakeholders. We are identifying available datasets and needs for additional data. We are analyzing data to specify the problems we're trying to solve.	We are designing and carrying out rigorous research on implementation and outcomes to inform local improvement efforts. We are building a data infrastructure. We are designing instruments that can inform their work.	We are focusing on the development of research evidence related to variability in implementation and outcomes and use this evidence internally in the educational system for continuous improvement.
Inform the work of others	We are identifying what new knowledge can be developed that also is relevant to practice. We are identifying potential strategies for organizing joint work.	We are sharing strategies for organizing our partnership work within professional networks doing similar work. We are adapting other partnerships' strategies for organizing our partnership.	We are sharing improvement strategies and results within professional networks of researchers and practitioners working on other problems of practice. Others are using our ideas, tools, or research evidence in their own work.

EXHIBIT 8

Who Should Be at the Table?

Healthy partnerships carefully organize themselves to balance power and participation equitably between institutions and between roles within institutions. This is particularly important when leadership decisions are deliberated, and in the design and implementation of the focal product of a partnership, such as a professional development program, curriculum, or afterschool program for youth.

The following is an example of some of the team structures in a Washington State Math Science Partnership Project—Partnership for Science and Engineering Practices (PSEP)—involving the Seattle Public Schools, the Renton School District, the Institute for Systems Biology (ISB), and the University of Washington Institute for Science and Math Education (UWISME). This partnership focuses on professional development for elementary- and middle-school science teachers, in which they learn to adapt their instruction to the recently adopted Next Generation Science Standards.

Use the study questions at the end to consider how you can organize your partnership for equitable participation.

Sample Team Structures

Leadership Team: *Meets quarterly to set course, monitor, and adjust*

- Seattle Public Schools: STEM director (principal investigator), science program manager, PSEP project manager
- Renton School District: Curriculum director (co-PI), science coach
- ISB: Education center director (co-PI)
- UWISME: Executive director (co-PI)
- External evaluator

Professional Development Design Team: *Develops and facilitates summer workshops and school-year release days*

- Seattle Public Schools: Science program manager, science coaches, PSEP project manager

- Renton School District: Science coach
- ISB: Professional development facilitator
- UWISME: Graduate students, postdoctoral fellows

Online Resources Team: *Organizes and publishes internal and external project resources*

- Seattle Public Schools: PSEP project manager
- ISB: Education center director, communications director
- UWISME: Executive director, graduate students, communications specialist

Research seminars: *Semiannually formally presents research; sets course*

- All project staff

Research check-ins: *Meets monthly to monitor and adjust course*

- Seattle Public Schools: Science program manager
- Renton School District: Science coach
- UWISME: Executive director, postdoctoral scholar

Study Questions

- How is representation balanced between the partner institutions in the project, and between roles within institutions in the project? How do you achieve balance in representation in your partnership?
- How can you include voices from different levels throughout the system, such as teachers and not just school district central-office administrators, when those people cannot all attend leadership meetings?
- Which functional groupings in your partnership require participation from all partners, and which can be handled by a subset?
- How do you structure participation to break down traditional institutional lines in your partnership—for example, how can practitioners influence research and how can researchers influence practitioners' work?

EXHIBIT 9

Promoting Equity Within a Partnership

Equity in a research-practice partnership means that all partners have shared interest and equal voice in the purpose, conduct, and outcomes of projects.

The following questions were developed by Jean Ryoo and Michelle Choi at the Exploratorium, and Emily McLeod at Techbridge. You can use these to help clarify meanings of equity up front in a partnership, structure engagement so that it is equitable among partners, and promote continual equity.

Questions for Ensuring Equity

Establishing Equity

Form an equitable foundation through organized discussions that build shared meaning and language.

- What do we mean by "equity" in educational opportunity and outcomes?
- What do we mean by "equity" in this partnership?

Identify expertise and sources of inequity that will shape relationships among partners.

- What experiences and expertise does each partner bring?
- How can we bring a greater diversity of skills, knowledge, and expertise to this group?
- How can we productively address issues of race, class, gender, sexuality, age, education, and experience?

Develop common definitions related to the work of the partnership.

- Do we have the same definitions for project aims and strategies?

Define shared project outcomes.

- What impact do we want our partnership to have?
- What will we know, be able to say, and understand as a result of working together?

Engaging Equitably

Decide how to engage participants equitably in the work, including decision making.

- Which activities will we engage in together, collaboratively?
- Who will be involved in what activities, and when and how will they be involved in these activities?
- How will decisions about the partnership, big and small, be made?

Decide how resources (both tangible and intellectual) will be distributed and allocated.

- How will time, money, and resources be divided across the partnership and how will this impact the work? (For example, the researcher(s) may have more time to review data but may want to involve educator partners in analysis. Can substitute teachers be paid for so educators can work with the partnership?)
- Who owns the intellectual work of the partnership, and how and when can it be shared?
- How and with whom will data be shared?
- How will partners be compensated for their contributions (e.g., meeting space, wages, meals, travel)?

Identify constraints on partners' engagement.

- What organizational and professional constraints on individuals' participation do we have to observe?
- What pressures, demands, and timeframes impact partners' professional lives and contexts (e.g., teaching responsibilities, school/organization policies and initiatives, evaluation and assessment)?

Encouraging Equity

Develop respectful processes for monitoring perspectives and responding to conflicts.

- What are our norms for communicating honestly and repairing relationships as needed?
- What modes of communication will best promote transparency and inclusive participation?
- What actions should we take to recognize when tensions arise and ensure respectful reconciliation?
- What are our "deal breakers" and "non-negotiables"?

Develop routines for reflecting on project and partnership progress.

- When should we check in about how our partnership is going?
- Are all partners getting what they need and want?
- How will we adjust course if necessary?

EXHIBIT 10

Deciding What to Prioritize in a Design Iteration

There is always room for improvement in our innovations, and there are never enough people or resources to make all the changes people want. Software developers use this template as a simple heuristic to help them set priorities about what bugs to fix and what features to add. Teams can work together in a research-practice partnership to fill out this template and set priorities for what improvements to make to address specific concerns or add components to an innovation. It is best to establish which concerns are important, and what features are most valued in a large group, with as wide a range of stakeholders as possible.

Decision-Making Template

Importance

Resources needed to address

High/High: Make a plan to address the concern or add components immediately.	**High/Low:** Address these concerns/needs last; identify possible workarounds, if the concern/need can't be addressed.
High/Low: Address the concern or add component immediately.	**Low/Low:** Address these concerns after high-importance concerns/needs have been addressed; identify possible workarounds, if the concern/need can't be addressed.

EXHIBIT 11

Defining Leadership Roles in Design

When partnerships engage in design work, it is important to define clear roles and responsibilities for each participant in the process. A participant's role should draw on their strengths, as well as on the respect they command within the team. The existing lines of authority with each organization should be considered as well.

Design Activities That Need Leaders

There are many important activities in design work that need people who can lead them. Here are a few:

- Recruiting participants to join a design team
- Applying techniques to develop empathy for people implementing an innovation
- Defining design principles
- Clarifying problems to be solved and identifying possible roadblocks to implementation
- Identifying a range of possible solutions
- Managing tensions and conflict on the team
- Soliciting and summarizing continuous input/feedback on how design is going
- Facilitating co-design process
- Developing the actual innovation (e.g., curriculum development)
- Managing a production timeline
- Implementing an innovation when it is new

A partnership's leadership team can follow these steps to assign individuals to lead such activities.

Steps to Assigning Leadership Roles

1. Take stock of participants' strengths.
   - What are the strengths of people relative to the tasks that need to be done?
   - What strengths do people want to develop, and what roles can they grow into?
   - Which people are likely to work well together?
   - What expertise needs to be added to the team, given the work ahead and who is available?
   - Are there resources to add team members?

2. Consider how others regard individuals.
   - Who is likely to have recognized status as an expert in an area and have credibility as an authorized leader of the team as a whole?
   - Do people with recognized status have authority within their own organization to allocate their own time for a leadership role?

3. Establish some norms for how roles will be coordinated.
   - Identify lines of formal authority.
   - Set expectations regarding communication and reporting that are important to respect in the design work.

4. Assign roles based on analysis in steps 1–3.

EXHIBIT 12

Ways Partners Can Support Each Other's Work

Researchers and educators can support one another's work, even when it is not directly in support of the partnership's joint aims. Helping one another in the following ways strengthens the relationships in the partnership. It can also indirectly help each partner. For example, many researchers view implementation as the job of educators. But in a partnership, there are a variety of ways that researchers can help with implementation. Many of these ways actually benefit researchers indirectly, too, in that they help researchers learn what conditions support and hinder implementation of innovations.

Educators' Work That Research Partners Can Support

- Co-design and co-lead professional development for teachers, as well as for central-office leaders and principals.
- Complement district technology support with technology support for new tools.
- Help teachers meet individual professional goals (e.g., national boards, future career opportunities) through participation in the partnership.
- Answer questions teachers, school, or district leaders have about research.
- Surface emerging tensions between the central office and schools, as well as people who might need extra help (e.g., run interference for teacher observations that go wrong).
- Be a sounding board for emerging problems, offering both practical advice but also identifying ideas from research.
- Quickly review literature related to an implementation problem that emerges.
- Broker relationships to other researchers with resources that the district might find useful.
- Identify appropriate research methods for systematically answering questions related to implementation.
- Help identify funding opportunities that are specific to particular questions or problems at hand when something is new to research.

Researchers' Work That Educator Partners Can Support

- Provide letters of support for grants that are more peripheral to the partnership.
- Write letters for tenure and promotion.
- Mentor graduate students on the ways of school districts.
- Broker access to other people in the educational organizations, both for your partner and people your partner vouches for.
- Broker access to research sites and participants peripheral to partnership work.
- Speak at research conferences with researcher partners (enhances the researcher's credibility as a good partner to educators).
- Give researchers the inside scoop on major initiatives (this makes them competitive within the district for resources linked to initiatives).

EXHIBIT 13

Whose Work Are We Doing?

In their article, "Design Experimentation and Mutual Appropriation: Two Strategies for University/Collaborative After-School Interventions," Deborah Downing-Wilson, Robert Lecusay, and Michael Cole underscore the value for partnerships of having a mix of different kinds of work.[3] *Some work researchers do solely to help their partner out—it's neither the partnership's joint work nor work researchers would do on their own if the partnership didn't exist. Other work is hybrid, building on some innovation that already existed in the education setting. The third category of work comprises new innovations the partners design and implement together.*

The following table gives examples from their article, which focused on a partnership between the University of California San Diego and a local Boys and Girls Club.

Category of work	Example
Activity that was part of the education partner's work, but not the researchers' work	Helping with tutoring at the club
Activity that was hybrid—it existed in the educational setting already, but researchers modified it	Helping build up the garden and improving the health value of snacks at the club
Activity that the partnership designed and implemented together	A science afterschool program

A Self-Assessment Tool for Researchers in a Partnership

Researchers can use this self-assessment tool to help diagnose the extent to which they are engaged in these different forms of work. We hypothesize that a healthy partnership has a mix of activities in each of these categories.

	Researcher activities	
	We've done this activity in the past	We're doing this activity now or planning to do it
Activities that are part of the education partner's work, but not the researchers' work.		
Activities that are hybrid: the activity existed in the educational setting, but researchers change it in some way through their activity.		
Activities to design and implement innovations together.		

EXHIBIT 14

Diagnosing the Health of Your Partnership in Difficult Times

Sometimes partnerships reach an impasse. The impasse may be due to strained relationships or to obstacles the partnership can't overcome to accomplish its goals. Partners need to answer some of these questions separately, and others they should discuss together, to diagnose the health of their partnership in difficult times. The diagnosis may result in a decision to alter the arrangement between the two partners (see exhibit 2, "What Kind of Collaboration Do We Want and Need?"). It may also result in a decision to take a break from the partnership or end it.

Questions to Answer on Your Own

About Your Relationship to the Partner

- If you often get annoyed at your partner organization, do you pause to determine what the problem is?
- Do you still value and appreciate the strengths and capabilities of the partner organization?
- Are the partner organization's needs and problems still of concern to you (i.e., addressing them is still worth it to you, because the partnership is still valuable to you)?
- Have the partner organization's needs and problems changed, such that the work you have been doing together fits the context of one of the organizations?
- Are you able to keep yourselves from driving an issue repeatedly to a painful point, without resolution?

If you answer no to one or more of these, your partnership might be in trouble.

About the Relationship of Self to the Work

- Is the work nearly always exhausting, or does it still energize and inspire you?
- Do you regularly "overcommit" to the work to meet partners' needs, even when you don't have time or resources to do so?

If you answer yes to one or both of these, your partnership might be in trouble.

Questions to Answer Together

- Are we meeting regularly, or have meetings dropped off in number and frequency? If we are meeting less regularly, is this because we've not felt the need or because we don't feel that meetings are productive?
- To what extent are the needs of each partner organization being met by the partnership?

If the answers to these questions are no, ask:

- Do we have the willingness and authority to adapt within the broad framework of the partnership's aims or to adjust the aims to better meet partners' needs?

If the answer is no, ask:

- Could the relationship change to some other collaborative agreement, such as one identified in chapter 2?

If the answer is no, ask:

- Might we need to go separate ways, at least temporarily? And is there a way to establish what conditions would reengage us as productive partners?

If the answer is yes, then set a timeline for check-in, based on the nature of precipitating events (e.g., pending outcome of some new reorganization or if new policy X evolves to not be constraining in ways that have led to an impasse in the work).

EXHIBIT 15

Check-in Routine for Partnership Meetings

Partnerships sustain themselves by routinely monitoring and responding to external and internal conditions that threaten their health. You can use the following set of questions to open your regularly scheduled partnership meetings. Participants can answer in whip-around fashion, with the group discussing more deeply when any responses raise concern.

Check-In Questions

1. What's happening in your institution?

Being aware of each other's context prevents surprises and allows the partnership to prepare for threats. Paying attention to what others focus on in both positive and negative responses to this question also helps partners continue to develop a sense of what matters to each other.

2. Are your personal needs being met through the partnership?

Partnerships demand energy of participants, and that is refueled by personal satisfaction with some aspect of the work. If participants' personal needs are not being met, their desire to keep up the work can quickly wane. This question also helps identify simple needs that can fester into big problems if not addressed. For example, if an individual prefers particular approaches to how communication or logistical matters are handled, norms for these can be developed.

3. Are your institution's needs being met through the partnership?

Partnerships must adapt continually to the evolving needs of their participating institutions. For example, if a school district has a new initiative under which all activities must fit, the partnership must justify its activities—and possibly its existence—in terms of that initiative.

4. Are we meeting our partnership's needs?

Mutualism, community, and overall healthy relationship features sustain partnerships. Additionally, partnerships usually carry commitments to external entities, such as a funder supporting the partnership's work on specific projects. If these commitments are not kept, the partnership risks losing material support for its existence.

EXHIBIT 16

Reviewing Data Together

A discussion of findings from a study can be a participatory activity that brings together perspectives of researchers and educators who were part of it. The discussion requires sensitivity to protocols for protecting the confidentiality of individual participants. It also requires a thoughtful approach to creating a level playing field for researchers and educators to share ideas, in which the wisdom of practice has a voice alongside data collected from observations, surveys, and interviews. The focus of a meeting should be formative, aimed at improving the efficacy of a design and its implementation.

A good question to frame such a discussion might be: What did we learn from implementing this innovation that can help us improve it?

This sample agenda was developed by Kerri Wingert and Shelley Stromholt at the University of Washington and William R. Penuel at the University of Colorado Boulder.

Meeting Agenda

Introductions

Share out something that we thought went well about implementation.

Set Goal and Norms for Session

Goal:

The aim is to share what we learned from direct observation, experience, and analysis of research protocols in order to improve our innovation.

Norms:

- Listen to all perspectives: the more we get on the table, the more robust our innovation will be in different contexts.
- The wisdom of experience and research evidence are both valuable sources of information.
- Seek to clarify points of confusion and embrace divergent perspectives.

"Writestorm" Observations

All participants write down on sticky notes as many different observations as they have about the implementation. Each note should have one idea. The idea could be an observation from a researcher or an experience of a participant. Examples include, "96% of teachers said the PD is valuable, and "I noticed my ELL students seem to have much higher engagement with modeling."

Post Observations on a Wall and Group Them

Once everyone has had a chance to write down at least 3–5 observations, post them on a large wall where similar ones can be grouped. Invite any participant to move a sticky note next to another one. Keep moving notes until the clustering feels complete. Some notes may still stand alone: these may be important ones, too. It may also be necessary or helpful for participants to explain what they wrote or to share their observations aloud.

The facilitator should ask the group to give a name to each cluster. Go for names in complete sentences, like, "Students were confused by the need to support their personal opinions with evidence from the text." Writing in complete sentences helps with knowing how to address an issue that arises.

Prioritize Clusters of Issues to Address

The group can use "sticky dots" to indicate which issues are most important to address in the next iteration of the innovation. Give each team about one-third the number of dots as are clusters of issues, so that the group has to prioritize problems.

After everyone has voted with dots, engage the group in a discussion of why these emerged as priorities. Understanding the "why" can deepen the discussion and help move the group to action.

Identify Action Steps

For the priority issues, identify at least 1–2 action steps to address them and decide who will be responsible for taking these steps. Make sure each step is doable and that it addresses the core goals of the project. Try to keep the perspectives of research and practice represented in these action teams.

For issues that are not at the top of the priority list, record them and set a time when the group will review them again, after the action steps identified have been taken.

Reflection

Ask the group to share something they learned by hearing from different perspectives during the session. This step reinforces the value of learning from one another.

EXHIBIT 17

Building Support for Research-Practice Partnerships

The potential value of research-practice partnerships varies by stakeholder group. Understanding these groups' concerns is key to persuading them to invest in a partnership approach to research and development. The following talking points are grounded in research on the dynamics and outcomes of successful partnerships, though they are certainly not true of all partnerships. You can use them as guides to craft a "pitch" to local or state policy makers or prospective partners that includes specifics of the investment you want someone to make in a partnership.

Talking Points for Local and State Policy Makers

- The involvement of external researchers in an improvement effort can give us a neutral, independent voice on its impacts.
- In a partnership, we can answer research questions we care about.
- Researchers are accountable to help us focus on our problems.
- We can trust researchers working in close partnership with us to be sensitive to political issues relevant to the district.
- Research partners can inform the design of complex policy initiatives with multiple moving parts.
- Research partners can help us identify evidence-based programs to implement that are a good fit to our district's or state's needs.
- Research partners help guide decisions about where to direct resources and funding for a problem for which no intervention currently exists.
- Research partners can conduct research during the development of a policy or initiative to help improve it.
- Research partners can inform the design of policies and requests for proposals for grant programs in ways that reflect research evidence for a given area.
- Access to researchers can strengthen messages to support particular initiatives.
- Research partners can share evidence with us from other states about how to bring things to scale at the level of a state.

Talking Points for Education Leader (Potential Partner)

- A research partner can help us to identify evidence-based programs to implement in a range of areas.
- A research partner brings resources (e.g., staffing, professional development design and delivery) to implement initiatives we already have going on.
- Research partners can help us to develop and test effective interventions that address problems of practice.
- Research partners can be thought partners on issues of concern to the district.
- Research partners can help broker access to others in the research world.

Talking Points for a Principal Investigator (Potential Research Partner)

- Education leaders are in a position to make an impact on practice that is informed by research.
- Education leaders can bring research alive, so that it does not just sit in a journal that few people read.
- The direct involvement of education leaders in research can make for more compelling grant proposals.
- The questions to ask in research will be more relevant and useful to educators you want to reach.

Notes

Foreword

1. See, for example, http://www.knaer-recrae.ca/blog-news-events/creating-partnerships-learning-new-ways-to-connect.

Chapter 1

1. http://ies.ed.gov/ncee/wwc/
2. William R. Penuel et al., *Findings from a National Survey of Research Use Among School and District Leaders* (Boulder, CO: National Center for Research in Policy and Practice, 2016).
3. Thomas B. Corcoran, Susan Fuhrman, and C. L. Belcher, "The District Role in Instructional Improvement," *Phi Delta Kappan* 83, no. 1 (2001): 78–84.
4. William R. Penuel et al., "What Research District Leaders Find Useful," *Educational Policy* (in press).
5. Jeremy Roschelle et al., "Integration of Technology, Curriculum, and Professional Development for Advancing Middle School Mathematics: Three Large-Scale Studies," *American Educational Research Journal* 47, no. 4 (2010): 833–78.
6. Robert K. Merton, "The Matthew Effect in Science," *Science* 159, no. 3810 (1968): 56–63.
7. Keith E. Stanovich, "Matthew Effects in Reading: Some Consequences of Individual Differences in the Acquisition of Literacy," *Reading Research Quarterly* 21, no. 4 (1986): 360–407; Herbert J. Walberg and Shiow-Ling Tsai, "Matthew Effects in Education," *American Educational Research Journal* 20, no. 3 (1983): 359–73.
8. Cynthia E. Coburn, William R. Penuel, and Kimberly Geil, *Research-Practice Partnerships at the District Level: A New Strategy for Leveraging Research for Educational Improvement* (Berkeley, CA and Boulder, CO: University of California and University of Colorado, 2013); Cynthia E. Coburn and William R. Penuel, "Research-Practice Partnerships in Education: Outcomes, Dynamics, and Open Questions," *Educational Researcher* 45, no. 1 (2016): 48–54.

9. Jeremy Roschelle, Jennifer Knudsen, and Stephen J. Hegedus, "From New Technological Infrastructures to Curricular Activity Systems: Advanced Designs for Teaching and Learning," in *Designs for Learning Environments of the Future: International Perspectives from the Learning Sciences*, ed. Michael J. Jacobson and Peter Reimann (New York: Springer, 2010), 233–62.
10. Ingrid A. Nelson, Rebecca A. London, and Karen R. Strobel, "Reinventing the Role of the University Researcher," *Educational Researcher* 44, no. 1 (2015): 17–26.
11. Penuel et al., "What Research District Leaders Find Useful."
12. Mary Kay Stein et al., "Algebra: A Challenge at the Crossroads of Policy and Practice," *Review of Educational Research* 81, no. 4 (2011): 453–92.
13. Harold E. Pashler et al., *Organizing Instruction and Study to Improve Student Learning: NCER 2007–2004* (Washington, DC: National Center for Education Research, Institute of Education Sciences, US Department of Education, 2007).
14. Julie L. Booth et al., "Design-Based Research Within the Constraints of Practice: AlgebraByExample," *Journal of Education for Students Placed at Risk* 20, no. 1–2 (2015): 79–100.
15. Coburn and Penuel, "Research-Practice Partnerships in Education."
16. William R. Penuel, Cynthia E. Coburn, and Dan Gallagher, "Negotiating Problems of Practice in Research-Practice Partnerships Focused on Design," in *Design-Based Implementation Research: Theories, Methods, and Exemplars, National Society for the Study of Education Yearbook*, ed. Barry J. Fishman et al. (New York: Teachers College Record, 2013), 237–55.
17. National Research Council, *How People Learn: Brain, Mind, Experience, and School* (Washington, DC: National Academy Press, 1999).
18. Hugh Burkhardt and Alan H. Schoenfeld, "Improving Educational Research: Toward a More Useful, More Influential, and Better-Funded Enterprise," *Educational Researcher* 32, no. 9 (2003): 3–14.

Chapter 2

1. Joshua L. Glazer and Donald J. Peurach, "School Improvement Networks as a Strategy for Large-Scale Education Reform: The Role of Educational Environments," *Educational Policy* 27 (2013): 676–710.
2. Linda S. Olson, *Why September Matters: Improving Student Attendance* (Baltimore: Baltimore Education Research Consortium, 2014).
3. Martha Abele Mac Iver and Douglas Mac Iver, *The Baltimore City Schools Middle School STEM Summer Program with Vex Robotics* (Baltimore: Baltimore Education Research Consortium, 2015).
4. Rachel E. Durham et al., "University–District Partnership Research to Understand College Readiness Among Baltimore City Students," *Journal of Education for Students Placed at Risk (JESPAR)* 20, no. 1–2 (2015): 120–40.
5. Ann L. Brown, "Design Experiments: Theoretical and Methodological Challenges in Creating Complex Interventions in Classroom Settings," *Journal of the Learning Sciences* 2, no. 2 (1992): 141–78; Alan Collins, "Toward a Design Science of Education," in *New Directions in Educational Technology*, ed. Eileen Scanlon and Timothy O'Shea (New York: Springer-Verlag, 1992), 15–22.

6. Paul A. Cobb et al., "Design Experiments in Educational Research," *Educational Researcher* 32, no. 1 (2003): 9–13; William A. Sandoval, "Conjecture Mapping: An Approach to Systematic Educational Design Research," *Journal of the Learning Sciences* 23, no. 1 (2014): 18–36.
7. Terry Anderson and Julie Shattuck, "Design-Based Research: A Decade of Progress in Education Research?" *Educational Researcher* 41, no. 1 (2012): 16–25.
8. William R. Penuel et al., "Organizing Research and Development at the Intersection of Learning, Implementation, and Design," *Educational Researcher* 40, no. 7 (2011): 331–37.
9. William R. Penuel, Jeremy Roschelle, and Nicole Shechtman, "Designing Formative Assessment Software with Teachers: An Analysis of the Co-Design Process," *Research and Practice in Technology Enhanced Learning* 2, no. 1 (2007): 51–74.
10. Jonathan A. Supovitz, "Situated Research Design and Methodological Choices in Formative Program Evaluation," in *Design-Based Implementation Research: Theories, Methods, and Exemplars, National Society for the Study of Education Yearbook*, ed. Barry J. Fishman et al. (New York: Teachers College Record, 2013), 372–99.
11. NGSS Lead States, *Next Generation Science Standards: For States, by States* (Washington, DC: National Academies Press, 2013).
12. National Research Council, *Guide to Implementing the Next Generation Science Standards* (Washington, DC: National Academies Press, 2015).
13. http://sciencemathpartnerships.org/tools/curriculum-adaptation-toolkit/
14. Anthony S. Bryk et al., *Learning to Improve: How America's Schools Can Get Better at Getting Better* (Cambridge, MA: Harvard University Press, 2015).
15. Douglas C. Engelbart, "Toward High-Performance Organizations: A Strategic Role for Groupware" (paper presented at the GroupWare '92 Conference, San Jose, California, August 1992).
16. C. J. McCannon, Marie W. Schall, and R. J. Perla, Planning for Scale: A Guide for Designing Large-Scale Improvement Initiatives—IHI Innovation Series White Paper (Cambridge, MA: Institute for Healthcare Innovation, 2008).
17. David Yeager et al., *Practical Measurement* (Palo Alto, CA: Carnegie Foundation for the Advancement of Teaching, 2013).
18. Ruth Curran Neild, personal communication, meeting of IES Knowledge Utilization Centers, October 16, 2015; Government Accounting Office, *Education Research: Further Improvements Needed to Ensure Relevance and Assess Dissemination Efforts, Report to the Committee on Education and the Workforce, House of Representatives* (Washington, DC: Government Accounting Office, 2013).
19. NGSS Lead States, Next Generation Science Standards.
20. Nonye M. Alozie et al., "Co-Designing Supports for Science Instruction: Lessons from a Research-Practice Partnership" (paper presented at the NARST Annual International Conference, Baltimore, Maryland, 2016), 3.

Chapter 3

1. National Research Council, A Framework for K–12 Science Education: Practices, Crosscutting Concepts, and Core Ideas (Washington, DC: National Research Council, 2012).

2. Caitlin Farrell and Cynthia E. Coburn. "Absorptive Capacity: A Conceptual Framework for Understanding District Central Office Learning," *Journal of Educational Change* (in press).
3. Jonathan A. Supovitz, "Melding Internal and External Support for School Improvement: How the District Role Changes When Working Closely with External Instructional Support Providers," *Peabody Journal of Education* 83, no. 3 (2008): 459–78.
4. Mary Catherine O'Connor and Sarah Michaels, "Aligning Academic Talk and Participation Status Through Revoicing: Analysis of a Classroom Discourse Strategy," *Anthropology and Education Quarterly* 24, no. 4 (1993): 318–55.
5. Michael L. Tushman and Thomas J. Scanlan, "Characteristics and External Orientations of Boundary Spanning Individuals," *Academy of Management Journal* 24, no. 1 (1981): 83–98.
6. Michael L. Tushman and Thomas J. Scanlan, "Boundary Spanning Individuals: Their Role in Information Transfer and Their Antecedents," *Academy of Management Journal* 24, no. 2 (1981): 289–305.
7. David R. Millen, "Rapid Ethnography: Time Deepening Strategies for HCI Field Research," in *Proceedings of the Conference on Designing Interactive Systems: Processes, Practices, Methods, and Techniques*, ed. Daniel Boyarski and Wendy A. Kellogg (New York: ACM Press, 2000), 280–86.
8. William R. Penuel, "Emerging Forms of Formative Intervention Research in Education," *Mind, Culture, and Activity* 21, no. 2 (2014): 97–117.
9. William R. Penuel and Barbara Means, "Using Large-Scale Databases in Evaluation: Advances, Opportunities, and Challenges," *American Journal of Evaluation* 32, no. 1 (2011): 118–33.
10. Anthony S. Bryk et al., *Learning to Improve: How America's Schools Can Get Better at Getting Better* (Cambridge, MA: Harvard University Press, 2015).
11. Ibid.
12. Yrjö Engeström et al., "Change Laboratory as a Tool for Transforming Work," *Lifelong Learning in Europe* 1, no. 2 (1996): 10–17.
13. Yrjö Engeström, Developmental Work Research: Expanding Activity Theory in Practice (Berlin: Lehmanns Media, 2005).
14. Annalisa Sannino, Annalisa, "Teachers' Talk of Experiencing: Conflict, Resistance and Agency," *Teaching and Teacher Education* 26, no. 4 (2010): 838–44.
15. Ibid.
16. Lisa Yamagata-Lynch and Sharon Smaldino, "Using Activity Theory to Evaluate and Improve K–12 School and University Partnerships," *Evaluation and Program Planning* 30, no. 4 (2007): 364–380.
17. http://researchandpractice.org/equitystory/

Chapter 4

1. Our definition of infrastructure is inspired by that of Leigh Star. See especially Susan Leigh Star, "The Ethnography of Infrastructure," *American Behavioral Scientist* 43, no. 3 (1999): 377–91.

2. Megan Bang et al., "Innovations in Culturally Based Science Education Through Partnerships and Community," in *New Science of Learning: Cognition, Computers, and Collaboration in Education*, ed. Myint Swe Khine and M. I. Saleh (New York: Springer, 2010), 569–92.
3. Ibid., 573.
4. Ingrid A. Nelson, Rebecca A. London, and Karen R. Strobel, "Reinventing the Role of the University Researcher," *Educational Researcher* 44, no. 1 (2015): 17–26.
5. Melissa Roderick, John Q. Easton, and Penny Bender Sebring, *The Consortium on Chicago School Research: A New Model for the Role of Research in Supporting Urban School Reform* (Chicago: Consortium on Chicago School Research, 2009).
6. Jeannie Oakes and John Rogers, "Radical Change Through Radical Means: Learning Power," *Journal of Educational Change* 8, no. 3 (2007): 193–206.
7. Ibid.
8. Thalia González, "Keeping Kids in Schools: Restorative Justice, Punitive Discipline, and the School to Prison Pipeline," *Journal of Law and Education* 41, no. 2 (2012): 281–335.
9. Yoli Anyon, personal e-mail communication, June 19, 2016.
10. Faith Connelly, Stephen Plank, and Tracy Rone, Baltimore Education Research Consortium: A Consideration of Past, Present, and Future (Baltimore: BERC, 2013), 1.
11. Ibid., 3.
12. https://www.nsf.gov/funding/pgm_summ.jsp?pims_id=503581
13. Samuel Severance, Heather Leary, and Raymond Johnson, "Tensions in a Multi-Tiered Research Partnership," in *Proceedings of the 11th International Conference of the Learning Sciences*, ed. Joseph L. Polman et al. (Boulder, CO: ISLS, 2014), 1171–75.
14. For a more detailed account of the design process, see Samuel Severance et al., "Organizing for Teacher Agency in Curricular Co-Design," *Journal of the Learning Sciences* (in press).
15. Deborah G. Ancona and David Caldwell, "Beyond Boundary Spanning: Managing External Dependence in Product Development Teams," *Journal of High Technology Management* 1, no. 2 (1990): 119–35; Daniela Damian, Irwin Kwan, and Sabrina Marczak, "Requirements-Driven Collaboration: Leveraging the Invisible Relationships Between Requirements and People," in *Collaborative Software Engineering*, ed. Ivan Mistrik et al. (Heidelberg, Germany: Springer, 2010), 57–76.
16. Göran Ekwall, "Creativity in Project Work: A Longitudinal Study of a Project Development Project," *Creativity and Innovation Management* 2, no. 1 (1993): 17–26; Martin Hoegl and Hans Georg Gemueden, "Teamwork Quality and the Success of Innovative Projects: A Theoretical Concept and Empirical Evidence," *Organization Science* 12, no. 4 (2001): 435–49.
17. Pernille Eskeröd, "The Human Resource Allocation Process When Organizing by Projects," in *Projects as Arenas for Renewal and Learning Processes*, ed. Rolf A. Lundin and Christophe Midler (Boston: Kluwer, 1998), 125–31.
18. Sanjiv Augustine et al., "Agile Project Management: Steering from the Edges," *Communications of the ACM* 48, no. 12 (2005): 85–89.
19. Severance et al., "Organizing for Teacher Agency in Curricular Co-Design."

20. Kavita Kapadia, Vanessa Coca, and John Q. Easton, *Keeping New Teachers: A First Look at the Influences of Induction in the Chicago Public Schools* (Chicago: Consortium on Chicago School Research, 2007).
21. Leah Sprain and David Boromisza-Habashi, "Meetings: A Cultural Perspective," *Journal of Multicultural Discourses* 7, no. 2 (2012): 179–89.

Chapter 5

1. Cynthia E. Coburn and Mary K. Stein, "Key Lessons About the Relationship Between Research and Practice," in *Research and Practice in Education: Building Alliances, Bridging the Divide*, ed. Cynthia E. Coburn and Mary K. Stein (Lanham, MD: Rowan & Littlefield, 2010), 201–26.
2. Anthony S. Bryk, "Accelerating How We Learn to Improve," *Educational Researcher* 44, no. 9 (2015): 467–77.
3. Anthony S. Bryk et al., *Learning to Improve: How America's Schools Can Get Better at Getting Better* (Cambridge, MA: Harvard University Press, 2015).
4. Susan Leigh Star, "This Is Not a Boundary Object: Reflections on the Origin of a Concept," *Science, Technology, and Human Values* 35, no. 5 (2010): 611.
5. Megan Hopkins et al., "Infrastructure Redesign and Instructional Reform in Mathematics," *Elementary School Journal* 114, no. 2 (2013): 200–24.
6. Hopkins et al., "Infrastructure Redesign"; James P. Spillane and Amy Franz Coldren, *Diagnosis and Design for School Improvement: Using a Distributed Perspective to Lead and Manage Change* (New York: Teachers College Press, 2010).
7. Geoffrey Bowker and Susan Leigh Star, *Sorting Things Out: Classification and Its Consequences* (Cambridge, MA: MIT Press, 1999).
8. Star, "This Is Not a Boundary Object."
9. William R. Penuel and James P. Spillane, "Learning Sciences and Policy Design and Implementation: Key Concepts and Tools for Collaborative Engagement," *in Cambridge Handbook of the Learning Sciences*, ed. R. Keith Sawyer (Cambridge, UK: Cambridge University Press, 2014), 649–67; Nora Sabelli, William R. Penuel, and Britte Haugan Cheng, "The Role of Informatics in Education Research and Policy," in *Governance in the Information Era: Theory and Practice of Policy Informatics*, ed. Erik W. Johnston (New York: Routledge, 2015), 213–28.
10. Star, "This Is Not a Boundary Object."
11. Spiro J. Maroulis et al., "Complex Systems View of Educational Policy Research," *Science* 330, no. 6000 (2010): 38–39.
12. Helena Karasti, "Infrastructuring in Participatory Design," in *Proceedings of the 13th Participatory Design Conference*, ed. Heike Winschiers-Theophilus, Vincenzo D'Andrea, and Ole Sejer Iversen (New York: Association of Computing Machinery, 2014), 141–50.
13. Christopher A. Le Dantec and Carl DiSalvo, "Infrastructuring and the Formation of Publics in Participatory Design," *Social Studies of Science* 43, no. 2 (2013): 241–64; Volkmar Pipek and Volker Wulf, "Infrastructuring: Toward an Integrated Perspective on the Design and Use of Information Technology," *Journal of the Association for Information Systems* 10 (May 2009): 447–73.

14. Elizabeth Covay and William Carbonaro, "After the Bell: Participation in Extracurricular Activities, Classroom Behavior, and Academic Achievement," *Sociology of Education* 83, no. 1 (2010): 20–45; National Research Council, *Identifying and Supporting Productive Stem Programs in Out-of-School Settings* (Washington, DC: National Research Council, 2015).
15. Elizabeth B.-N. Sanders and Pieter Jan Stappers, "Co-Creation and the New Landscapes of Design," *Co-design* 4, no. 1 (2008): 5–18.
16. William R. Penuel, Jeremy Roschelle, and Nicole Shechtman, "Designing Formative Assessment Software with Teachers: An Analysis of the Co-Design Process," *Research and Practice in Technology Enhanced Learning* 2, no. 1 (2007): 51–74.
17. Megan Bang and Shirin Vossoughi, "Participatory Design Research and Educational Justice: Studying Learning and Relations within Social Change Making," *Cognition and Instruction* 34, no. 3 (2016): 173–93.
18. Penuel et al., "Designing Formative Assessment Software with Teachers."
19. Pelle Ehn, "Scandinavian Design: On Participation and Skill," in *Usability: Turning Technologies into Tools*, ed. Paul S. Adler and Terry A. Winograd (New York: Oxford University Press, 1992), 96–132.
20. http://www.designkit.org/methods/28
21. Ian F. Alexander and Neil Maiden, *Scenarios, Stories, Use Cases* (New York: Wiley, 2004).
22. John M. Carroll, "Five Reasons for Scenario-Based Design," *Interacting with Computers* 13, no. 1 (2000): 43–60.
23. Ibid.
24. Joanna Weidler-Lewis and Sean Fullerton, "The Coaching Companion: Computer-Mediated Instructional Coaching," in *CSCW 2015 Companion* (New York: ACM, 2015), 251–54.
25. Henry Sanoff, Community Participation Methods in Planning and Design (New York: Wiley, 2000).
26. Dixie Ching et al., On-Ramps, Lane Changes, Detours and Destinations: Building Connected Learning Pathways in Hive NYC Through Brokering Future Learning Opportunities (New York: Hive Research Lab, 2015).
27. Greg J. Duncan and Richard J. Murnane, eds., *Whither Opportunity? Rising Inequality, Schools, and Children's Life Chances* (New York: Russell Sage Foundation, 2011).
28. Ching et al., On-Ramps, Lane Changes, Detours and Destinations.
29. Robert A. Virzi, "Refining the Test Phase of Usability Evaluation: How Many Subjects Is Enough?" *Human Factors* 34, no. 4 (1992): 457–368.
30. Jere Confrey et al., "Equipartitioning/Splitting as a Foundation of Rational Number Reasoning Using Learning Trajectories," in *Proceedings of the 33rd Conference of the International Group for the Psychology of Mathematics Education*, ed. Marianna Tzekaki, Maria Kaldrimidou, and Haralambos Sakonidis (Thessaloniki, Greece: PME, 2009), 345–52.
31. Christine Zanchi, Ashley Lewis Presser, and Philip Vahey, "Next Generation Preschool Math Demo: Tablet Games for Preschool Classrooms," in *Proceedings of Interaction Design and Children 2013*, ed. Juan Pablo Hourcade, Nitin Sawhney, and Emily Reardon (New York: ACM, 2013), 527–30.

32. A theory of participatory design called *adversarial design* is well suited for such situations. For more about this theory, see Carl DiSalvo, *Adversarial Design* (Cambridge, MA: MIT Press, 2012).
33. Raymond Johnson et al., "Teachers, Tasks, and Tensions: Lessons from a Research-Practice Partnership," *Journal of Mathematics Teacher Education* 19, no. 2 (2016): 169–85.
34. Sepehr Vakil et al., "Rethinking Race and Power in Design-Based Research: Reflections from the Field," *Cognition and Instruction* 34, no. 3 (2016): 194–209.

Chapter 6

1. Joshua L. Glazer and Donald J. Peurach, "School Improvement Networks as a Strategy for Large-Scale Education Reform: The Role of Educational Environments," *Educational Policy* 27, no. 4 (2013): 676–710.
2. Geoffrey D. Borman et al., "Comprehensive School Reform and Achievement: A Meta-Analysis," *Review of Educational Research* 73, no. 2 (2003): 125–230; Jonathan A. Supovitz and Henry May, "A Study of the Links Between Implementation and Effectiveness of the America's Choice Comprehensive School Reform Design," *Journal of Education for Students Placed at Risk (JESPAR)* 9, no. 4 (2004): 389–419.
3. Glazer and Peurach, "School Improvement Networks."
4. Geoffrey D. Borman et al., "Success for All: First-Year Results from the National Randomized Field Trial," *Educational Evaluation and Policy Analysis* 27, no. 1 (2005): 1–22.
5. National Research Council, *Using Science as Evidence in Public Policy* (Washington, DC: The National Academies Press, 2012).
6. Michael Cole and the Distributed Literacy Consortium, *The Fifth Dimension: An After-School Program Built on Diversity* (Beverly Hills, CA: Sage, 2006).
7. Angelici Nicolopoulou and Michael Cole, "The Fifth Dimension, Its Play-World, and Its Institutional Context: Generation and Transmission of Shared Knowledge in the Culture of Collaborative Learning," in *Context for Learning: Sociocultural Dynamics in Children's Development*, ed. Elyse A. Forman, Nirris Minick, and C. Addison Stone (New York: Oxford University Press, 1993), 283–314.
8. Daniela DiGiacomo and Kris D. Gutiérrez, "Relational Equity as a Design Tool Within Making and Tinkering Activities," *Mind, Culture, and Activity* 23, no. 2 (2016): 141–53.
9. For more data on the effectiveness of the Fifth Dimension design, see William Blanton et al., "Effects of Participation in the Fifth Dimension on Far Transfer," *Journal of Educational Computing Research* 16, no. 4 (1997): 371–96.
10. A. Susan Jurow, "Cultivating Self in the Context of Transformative Professional Development," *Journal of Teacher Education* 60, no. 3 (2009): 277--90.
11. Noah D. Finkelstein, "Teaching and Learning Physics: A Model for Coordinating Physics Instruction, Outreach, and Research," *Journal of Scholarship of Teaching and Learning* 4, no. 2 (2004): 1–17.
12. The use of the term "mangle" here is a reference to Andrew Pickering's *The Mangle of Practice: Time, Agency, and Science* (Chicago: University of Chicago Press, 1995).
13. Joseph A. Durlak et al., "The Impact of Enhancing Students' Social and Emotional Learning: A Meta-Analysis of School-Based Universal Interventions," *Child Development* 82, no. 1 (2011): 405–32.

14. Deborah Downing-Wilson, Robert Lecusay, and Michael Cole, "Design Experimentation and Mutual Appropriation: Two Strategies for University/Collaborative After-School Interventions," *Theory & Psychology* 21, no. 5 (2011): 656–80.
15. Nicolopoulou and Cole, "The Fifth Dimension"; Downing-Wilson et al., "Design Experimentation and Mutual Appropriation."
16. Brian Rowan and Cecil G. Miskel, "Institutional Theory and the Study of Educational Organizations," in *Handbook of Research on Educational Administration*, ed. Jerome Murphy and Karen S. Louis (San Francisco: Jossey-Bass, 1999), 359–84; Brian Rowan, "Commitment and Control: Alternative Strategies for the Organizational Design of Schools," in *Review of Research in Education*, ed. Courtney Cazden (Washington, DC: AERA, 1990), 353–89.
17. Raymond Johnson et al., "Teachers, Tasks, and Tensions: Lessons from a Research-Practice Partnership," *Journal of Mathematics Teacher Education* 19, no. 2 (2016): 169–85.
18. Tamara Sumner and the Curriculum Customization Service Team, "Customizing Instruction with Educational Digital Libraries," in *Proceedings of the 10th Annual Joint Conference on Digital Libraries*, ed. Jane Hunter et al. (New York: Association for Computing Machinery, 2010), 353–56.
19. Douglas H. Clements and Julie Sarama, "Learning Trajectories in Mathematics Education," *Mathematical Thinking and Learning* 6, no. 2 (2004): 81–90; Martin A. Simon, "Reconstructing Mathematics Pedagogy from a Constructivist Perspective," *Journal for Research in Mathematics Education* 26, no. 2 (1995): 114–45.
20. William R. Penuel et al., "What Makes Professional Development Effective? Strategies That Foster Curriculum Implementation," *American Educational Research Journal* 44, no. 4 (2007): 921–58.
21. William R. Penuel and Louise Yarnall, "Designing Handheld Software to Support Classroom Assessment: An Analysis of Conditions for Teacher Adoption," *Journal of Technology, Learning, and Assessment* 3, no. 5 (2005).
22. Louise Yarnall, Nicole Shechtman, and William R. Penuel, "Using Handheld Computers to Support Improved Classroom Assessment in Science: Results from a Field Trial," *Journal of Science Education and Technology* 15, no. 2 (2006): 142–58.
23. Phyllis Blumenfeld et al., "Creating Usable Innovations in Systemic Reform: Scaling Up Technology-Embedded Project-Based Science in Urban Schools," *Educational Psychologist* 35, no. 3 (2000): 149–64; Glazer and Peurach, "School Improvement Networks."
24. David K. Cohen et al., *Improvement by Design: The Promise of Better Schools* (Chicago: University of Chicago Press, 2013).
25. Mary Kay Stein et al., Implementing Standards-Based Mathematics Instruction: A Casebook for Professional Development (New York: Teachers College Press, 2009).
26. Donald J. Peurach, "Innovating at the Nexus of Impact and Improvement: Leading Educational Improvement Networks," *Educational Researcher* 45, no. 7 (2016): 421–29.
27. Anthony S. Bryk et al., *Learning to Improve: How America's Schools Can Get Better at Getting Better* (Cambridge, MA: Harvard University Press, 2015).
28. Maggie Hannan, "Adaptive Integration in the BTEN Network" (paper presented at the Annual Meeting of the American Educational Research Association, Washington, DC, April 2016).

29. Aasha Joshi and William R. Penuel, "The Role of Institutionalized Norms of Autonomy and Equality in Shaping Interactions of Teachers" (paper presented at the 4th Lake Arrowhead Conference on Human Complex Systems, Lake Arrowhead, CA, April 2007); Judith Warren Little, "The Persistence of Privacy: Autonomy and Initiative in Teachers' Professional Relations," *Teachers College Record* 91, no. 4 (1990): 129–51.
30. Cynthia E. Coburn and Jennifer L. Russell, "District Policy and Teachers' Social Networks," *Educational Evaluation and Policy Analysis* 30, no. 3 (2008): 203–35; Kenneth A. Frank, Yong Zhao, and Kathryn Borman, "Social Capital and the Diffusion of Innovations Within Organizations: Application to the Implementation of Computer Technology in Schools," *Sociology of Education* 77, no. 2 (2004): 148–71; Milbrey W. McLaughlin and Joan E. Talbert, *Professional Communities and the Work of High School Teaching* (Chicago: University of Chicago Press, 2001); William R. Penuel et al., "Using Social Network Analysis to Study How Collegial Interactions Can Augment Teacher Learning from External Professional Development," *American Journal of Education* 119, no. 1 (2012): 103–36.

Chapter 7

1. Anne L. Garrison, "Understanding Teacher and Contextual Factors That Influence the Enactment of Cognitively Demanding Mathematics Tasks" (PhD diss. Vanderbilt University, 2013).
2. See, for example, William R. Penuel et al., "Impact of Project-Based Curriculum Materials on Student Learning in Science: Results of a Randomized Controlled Trial," *Journal of Research in Science Teaching* 52, no. 10 (2015): 1362–85.
3. Laura D'Amico, "The Center for Learning Technologies in Urban Schools: Evolving Relationships in Design-Based Research," in *Research and Practice in Education: Building Alliances, Bridging the Divide*, ed. Cynthia E. Coburn and Mary K. Stein (Lanham, MD: Rowan & Littlefield, 2010), 37–53.
4. Ibid.
5. Institute of Education Sciences and National Science Foundation, *Common Guidelines for Education Research and Development* (Washington, DC: IES and NSF, 2013).
6. Barbra Beck et al., "Funding Setbacks: Partnership Strategies for Success," *Metropolitan Universities* 11, no. 2 (2000): 11–19.
7. Ibid.
8. William R. Penuel, Jeremy Roschelle, and Nicole Shechtman, "Designing Formative Assessment Software with Teachers: An Analysis of the Co-Design Process," *Research and Practice in Technology Enhanced Learning* 2, no. 1 (2007): 51–74.
9. William R. Penuel and Louise Yarnall, "Designing Handheld Software to Support Classroom Assessment: An Analysis of Conditions for Teacher Adoption," *Journal of Technology, Learning, and Assessment* 3, no. 5 (2005).
10. Koeno Gravemeijer and Paul Cobb, "Design Research from a Learning Design Perspective," in *Educational Design Research*, ed. Jan van den Akker et al. (New York: Routledge, 2013), 73–112.

Chapter 8

1. Melissa Roderick, John Q. Easton, and Penny Bender Sebring, *The Consortium on Chicago School Research: A New Model for the Role of Research in Supporting Urban School Reform* (Chicago: Consortium on Chicago School Research, 2009).
2. Ibid., 9.
3. Yvonna S. Lincoln and Egon G. Guba, *Naturalistic Inquiry* (Thousand Oaks, CA: Sage, 1985).
4. Roderick et al., The Consortium on Chicago School Research, 7.
5. Ben Kirshner, "Productive Tensions in Youth Participatory Action Research, in *Learning Research as a Human Science. National Society for the Study of Education Yearbook*, ed. William R. Penuel and Kevin O'Connor, (New York: Teachers College Record), 238–51.
6. William R. Penuel et al., *Findings from a National Survey of Research Use Among School and District Leaders* (Boulder, CO: National Center for Research in Policy and Practice, 2016).
7. Carol H. Weiss and Michael J. Bucuvalas, *Social Science Research and Decision-Making* (New York: Columbia University Press, 1980).
8. Raymond S. Nickerson, "Confirmation Bias: A Ubiquitous Phenomenon in Many Guises," *Review of General Psychology* 2, no. 2 (1998): 175–220.
9. National Research Council, Improving Student Learning: A Strategic Plan for Education Research and Its Utilization (Washington, DC: National Research Council, 1999).
10. The National Research Council report did not frame these as categories of research questions, but as types of research knowledge that should be accumulated and synthesized to inform practice. Additional types of knowledge highlighted in the original report include: knowledge about the strengths of the existing research base on different topics, knowledge of barriers and supports of research utilization, and knowledge of priorities of a network of educators and researchers engaged in knowledge building for practice.
11. Randy Elliot Bennett, "Formative Assessment: A Critical Review," *Assessment in Education: Principles, Policy, and Practices* 18, no. 1 (2011): 5–25; Paul Black and Dylan Wiliam, "Assessment and Classroom Learning," *Assessment in Education* 5, no. 1 (1998): 7–74; Terence J. Crooks, "The Impact of Classroom Evaluation Practices on Students," *Review of Educational Research* 58, no. 4 (1988): 438–81; Neal Kingston and Brooke Nash, "Formative Assessment: A Meta-Analysis and a Call for Research," *Educational Measurement: Issues and Practice* 30, no. 4 (2011): 28–37.
12. William R. Penuel and Lorrie A. Shepard, "Assessment and Teaching," in *Handbook of Research on Teaching*, ed. Drew H. Gitomer and Courtney A. Bell (Washington, DC: AERA, 2016), 787–851.
13. Paul Black and Dylan Wiliam, "Inside the Black Box: Raising Standards Through Classroom Assessment," *Phi Delta Kappan* 80, no. 2 (1998): 81–90.
14. William R. Penuel and Lawrence P. Gallagher, "Preparing Teachers to Design Instruction for Deep Understanding in Middle School Earth Science," *Journal of the Learning Sciences* 18, no. 4 (2009): 461–508.

15. Erin Marie Furtak et al., "On the Fidelity of Implementing Embedded Formative Assessment and Its Relation to Student Learning," *Applied Measurement in Education* 21, no. 4 (2008): 360–89.
16. James Hiebert and Diana Wearne, "Instructional Tasks, Classroom Discourse, and Students' Learning in Second-Grade Arithmetic," *American Educational Research Journal* 30, no. 2 (1993): 393–425; Mary Kay Stein and Suzanne Lane, "Instructional Tasks and the Development of Student Capacity to Think and Reason: An Analysis of the Relationship Between Teaching and Learning in a Reform Mathematics Project," *Educational Research and Evaluation* 2, no. 1 (1996): 50–80.
17. Mary Kay Stein et al., *Implementing Standards-Based Mathematics Instruction: A Casebook for Professional Development* (New York: Teachers College Press, 2009); Melissa D. Boston and Margaret S. Smith, "A 'Task-Centric Approach' to Professional Development: Enhancing and Sustaining Mathematics Teachers' Ability to Implement Cognitively Challenging Mathematical Tasks," *ZDM* 43, no. 6 (2011): 965–77.
18. Raymond Johnson et al., "Teachers, Tasks, and Tensions: Lessons from a Research-Practice Partnership," *Journal of Mathematics Teacher Education* 19, no. 2 (2016): 169–85.
19. David Yeager and Gregory M. Walton, "Social-Psychological Interventions in Education: They're Not Magic," *Review of Educational Research* 81, no. 2 (2011): 267–301.
20. Chris Hulleman and David S. Cordray, "Moving from the Lab to the Field: The Role of Fidelity and Achieved Relative Intervention Strength," *Journal of Research on Educational Effectiveness* 2, no. 1 (2009): 88–110.
21. David Paunesku et al., "Mind-Set Interventions Are a Scalable Treatment for Academic Underachievement," *Psychological Science* 26 (April 2015): 784–93.
22. Barry J. Fishman et al., "Comparing the Impact of Online and Face-to-Face Professional Development in the Context of Curriculum Implementation," *Journal of Teacher Education* 64, no. 5 (2013): 426–38.
23. Heather C. Hill, Mary Beisiegel, and Robin Jacob, "Professional Development Research: Consensus, Crossroads, and Challenges," *Educational Researcher* 42, no. 9 (2013): 476–87.
24. Carol L. O'Donnell, "Defining, Conceptualizing, and Measuring Fidelity of Implementation and Its Relationship to Outcomes in K–12 Curriculum Intervention Research," *Review of Educational Research* 78, no. 1 (2008): 33–84.
25. Joke M. Voogt et al., "Collaborative Design as a Form of Professional Development," *Instructional Science* 43, no. 2 (2015): 259–82.
26. Penuel and Gallagher, "Preparing Teachers to Design Instruction"; William R. Penuel, Lawrence P. Gallagher, and Savitha Moorthy, "Preparing Teachers to Design Sequences of Instruction in Earth Science: A Comparison of Three Professional Development Programs," *American Educational Research Journal* 48, no. 4 (2011): 996–1025.
27. Nicholas M. Kochmanski, Erin Craig Henrick, and Paul A. Cobb, "On the Development of Content-Specific Practical Measures Assessing Aspects of Instruction Associated with Student Learning" (paper presented at the Conference on Using Continuous Improvement to Integrating Design, Implementation, and Scale Up, Nashville, TN, October 8–9, 2015).

28. Elaine Allensworth, "The Use of Ninth-Grade Early Warning Indicators to Improve Chicago Schools," *Journal of Education for Students Placed at Risk* 18, no. 1 (2015): 68–83; Elaine Allensworth and John Q. Easton. *The On-Track Indicator as a Predictor of High School Graduation* (Chicago: Consortium on Chicago School Research, 2005); Melissa Roderick et al., *Preventable Failure: Improvements in Long-Term Outcomes When High Schools Focused on the Ninth Grade Year* (Chicago: Consortium on Chicago School Research, 2014).
29. James J. Kemple, Micha D. Segeritz, and Nickisha Stephenson, "Building On-Track Indicators for High School Graduation and College Readiness: Evidence from New York City," *Journal of Education for Students Placed at Risk (JESPAR)* 18, no. 1 (2013): 7–28.
30. William R. Penuel et al., *Findings from a National Survey of Research Use Among School and District Leaders* (Boulder, CO: National Center for Research in Policy and Practice, 2016).
31. Anthony S. Bryk et al., eds., *Organizing Schools for Improvement: Lessons from Chicago* (Chicago: University of Chicago Press), 2010.
32. William R. Penuel et al., "What Research District Leaders Find Useful," *Educational Policy* (in press).
33. Yolanda Anyon et al., "The Persistent Effect of Race and the Promise of Alternatives to Suspension in School Discipline Outcomes," *Children and Youth Services Review* 44 (September 2014): 379–86.
34. William R. Penuel et al., "Students' Responses to Curricular Activities as Indicator of Coherence in Project-Based Science," in *Proceedings of the 12th International Conference of the Learning Sciences*, ed. Chee-Kit Looi et al. (Singapore: International Society of the Learning Sciences, 2016), 855–58.
35. Heather Johnson, "Project-Based Teaching: Helping Students Make Project Connections" (Ph.D. diss., Northwestern University, 2009); Virginia M. Pitts, "Do Students Buy In? A Study of Goal and Role Adoption by Students in Project-Based Curricula" (Ph.D. diss., Northwestern University, 2006).
36. Paul A. Cobb et al., "Design Research with Educational Systems: Investigating and Supporting Improvements in the Quality of Mathematics Teaching at Scale," in *Design-Based Implementation Research: Theories, Methods, and Exemplars. National Society for the Study of Education Yearbook,* ed. Barry J. Fishman et al. (New York: Teachers College Record, 2013), 320–49.
37. For a sample feedback report, see http://peabody.vanderbilt.edu/docs/pdf/tl/C_text_Redacted_Feedback_Report_2011.pdf
38. The report series can be found at http://math.sri.com.
39. Roderick et al., Consortium on Chicago School Research.
40. Ibid., 10.

Chapter 9

1. Ron Marx, "Large-Scale Interventions in Science Education: The Road to Utopia?" *Journal of Research in Science Teaching* 49, no. 3 (2012): 420–27.

2. Hugh Burkhardt and Alan H. Schoenfeld, "Improving Educational Research: Toward a More Useful, More Influential, and Better-Funded Enterprise," *Educational Researcher* 32, no. 9 (2003): 3–14.
3. Donald E. Stokes, *Pasteur's Quadrant: Basic Science and Technological Innovation* (Washington, DC: Brookings Institution, 1997).
4. National Research Council, *Strategic Education Research Partnership* (Washington, DC: National Research Council, 2003).
5. Megan Bang et al., "Innovations in Culturally Based Science Education Through Partnerships and Community," in *New Science of Learning: Cognition, Computers, and Collaboration in Education*, ed. Myint Swe Khine and M. I. Saleh (New York: Springer, 2010), 569–92.
6. Anthony S. Bryk, "Support a Science of Performance Improvement," *Phi Delta Kappan* 90, no. 8 (2009): 597–600.
7. For a review of these and possible applications to education research, see William R. Penuel and Barry J. Fishman, "Large-Scale Intervention Research We Can Use," *Journal of Research in Science Teaching* 49, no. 3 (2012): 281–304.
8. Jeffrey A. Kelly et al., "Bridging the Gap Between the Science and Service of HIV Prevention: Transferring Effective Research-Based HIV Prevention Interventions to Community AIDS Service Providers," *American Journal of Public Health* 90, no. 7 (2000): 1082; Margaret C. Watson et al., "Educational Strategies to Promote Evidence-Based Community Pharmacy Practice: A Cluster Randomized Controlled Trial," *Family Practice* 19, no. 5 (2002): 529–36.
9. Anthony S. Bryk et al., *Learning to Improve: How America's Schools Can Get Better at Getting Better* (Cambridge, MA: Harvard University Press, 2015).
10. Philip A. Woods and Peter Gronn, "Nurturing Democracy the Contribution of Distributed Leadership to a Democratic Organizational Landscape," *Educational Management Administration & Leadership* 37, no. 4 (2009): 430–51.
11. Michael E. Gorman, Trading Zones and Interactional Expertise: Creating New Kinds of Collaboration (Cambridge, MA: MIT Press, 2010); Scott Page, The Difference: How the Power of Diversity Creates Better Groups, Firms, Schools, and Societies (Princeton, NJ: Princeton University Press, 2008).
12. Philip Bell et al., "Researchers and Practitioners Co-Designing for Expansive Science Learning and Educational Equity," in *Proceedings of the 12th International Conference of the Learning Sciences*, ed. Chee-Kit Looi et al., (Singapore: International Society of the Learning Sciences, 2016), 1128–35.
13. National Research Council, Strategic Education Research Partnership.
14. Burkhardt and Schoenfeld, "Improving Educational Research"; M. Suzanne Donovan, "Generating Improvement Through Research and Development in Educational Systems," *Science* 340, no. 6130 (2013): 317–19.
15. KerryAnn O'Meary, Timothy Eatman, and Saul Peterson, "Advancing Engaged Scholarship in Promotion and Tenure: A Roadmap and Call for Reform," *Liberal Education* 101, no. 3 (2015): 52–57.

16. Susan P. Sturm, “The Architecture of Inclusion: Advancing Workplace Equity in Higher Education,” *Harvard Journal of Law and Gender* 29, no. 2 (2006): 248–334.
17. Ibid.
18. Jeffrey R. Henig, “The Politics of Data Use,” *Teachers College Record* 114, no. 11 (2012): 1–17.
19. William R. Penuel et al., *Findings from a National Survey of Research Use Among School and District Leaders* (Boulder, CO: National Center for Research in Policy and Practice, 2016).
20. Jane Hemsley-Brown and Caroline Sharp, “The Use of Research to Improve Professional Practice: A Systematic Review of the Literature,” *Oxford Review of Education* 29, no. 4 (2003): 449–70; Carol A. Dwyer, Catherine M. Millett, and David G. Payne, *A Culture of Evidence: Postsecondary Assessment and Learning Outcomes. Recommendations to Policymakers and the Higher Education Community* (Princeton, NJ: Educational Testing Service, 2006); Kate Gerrish and Jane Clayton, “Promoting Evidence-Based Practice: An Organizational Approach,” *Journal of Nursing Management* 12, no. 2 (2004): 114–23; Emma Fitzsimmons and Joanne Cooper, “Embedding a Culture of Evidence-Based Practice,” *Nursing Management* 19, no. 7 (2012): 14–19.
21. Penuel et al., Findings from a National Survey.
22. William R. Penuel et al., “What Research District Leaders Find Useful,” *Educational Policy* (in press).
23. Donovan, “Generating Improvement.”
24. David K. Cohen, *Teaching and Its Predicaments* (Cambridge, MA: Harvard University Press, 2011).
25. National Research Council, Strategic Education Research Partnership.
26. Brigid Barron, “Interest and Self-Sustained Learning as Catalysts of Development: A Learning Ecology Perspective,” *Human Development* 49, no. 4 (2006): 193–224; National Research Council, *Identifying and Supporting Productive STEM Programs in Out-of-School Settings* (Washington, DC: National Research Council, 2015).
27. John H. Falk et al., “The Synergies Research-Practice Partnership Project: A 2020 Vision Case Study,” *Cultural Studies of Science Education* 11, no. 1 (2016): 195–212.
28. Michelle Renée, Kevin Welner, and Jeannie Oakes, “Social Movement Organizing and Equity-Focused Educational Change: Shifting the Zone of Mediation,” in *Second International Handbook of Educational Change*, ed. Andrew Hargreaves et al. (London: Kluwer, 2009), 158–63.
29. Shelley Pasnik and Carlin Llorente, Preschool Teachers Can Use a PBS Kids Transmedia Curriculum Supplement to Support Young Children’s Mathematics Learning: Results of a Randomized Controlled Trial. A Report to the CPB-PBS Ready to Learn Initiative (Waltham, MA and Menlo Park, CA: EDC and SRI International, 2013); William R. Penuel et al., “Supplementing Literacy Instruction with a Media-Rich Intervention: Results of a Randomized Controlled Trial,” Early Childhood Research Quarterly 27, no. 1 (2012): 115–27.
30. Anna-Ruth Allen and Kristen L. Davidson, *Building Capacity for Research-Practice Partnerships: Needs and Strategies* (Boulder, CO: Research+Practice Collaboratory, 2015).
31. http://bit.ly/RPPForum

32. We owe credit for this image of gatherings of partnerships from Donald Peurach of the University of Michigan.

Appendix

1. http://www.frameworksinstitute.org/assets/files/evidence_implementation/NIRNreport_justdoit_2015.pdf
2. Bronwyn Bevan et al., *Enriching and Expanding the Possibilities of Research-Practice Partnerships in Informal Science* (San Francisco: The Exploratorium, 2015).
3. Deborah Downing-Wilson, Robert Lecusay, and Michael Cole, "Design Experimentation and Mutual Appropriation: Two Strategies for University/Collaborative After-School Interventions," *Theory & Psychology* 21, no. 5 (2011): 656–80.

Acknowledgments

This work is first and foremost informed by and indebted to our team members and partners, from whom we are learning continuously. For Bill, these include current and past members of the Inquiry Hub research team: Tamara Sumner, Katie Van Horne, Raymond Johnson, David Quigley, Heather Leary, and Sam Severance of the University of Colorado Boulder; Holly Devaul and Jonathan Oswald of the University Corporation for Atmospheric Research; Anne Westbrook and Connie Hvidsten of BSCS; Cathy Martin, Patty Kincaid, Jeff Miller, Douglas Watkins, Jennifer Yacoubian, and Becky Sauer of the Denver Public Schools' central office; and our many teacher co-designers in Denver Public Schools: Vicki Brown, Jackie Carillo, Arlene Friend, Kevin Lindauer, Jess Taylor, Ally Orwig, Bill Weisberger, Maria Manacheril, Ian Kearns, Kirk Hammond, Lisa Yemma, Anna Holm, Nancy Anderson, Megan Lawson, Mary Laves, Anna Paschke, Jennifer Reinert, Zach Rowe, Nick Steinmetz, Wendy Turner, Julie Stremel, and Michael Kraft.

Bill thanks Cynthia Coburn, who coauthored chapter 2 of this book, and our amazing team of researchers, who have been studying research-practice partnerships with support from the William T. Grant Foundation, the Institute of Education Sciences, and the Spencer Foundation. Thanks especially to Caitlin Farrell, Annie Allen, and Kristen Davidson (again, for their contributions to this effort), Melia Repko-Erwin, and Liah Bendix. Many of the research findings and some of the accounts presented here are based on insights and findings from our joint research.

Bill also wishes to call out Jeremy Roschelle for his mentorship and colleagueship in both the theory and practice of collaborative design, and the faculty of the Design-Based Implementation Research workshop for their support and leadership in breaking new ground in the learning sciences for working in and writing about research-practice partnerships: Barry Fishman, Tiffany Clark, Phil Bell (again), Alicia Grunow, Nichole Pinkard, and Jennifer Russell. He also calls out Dean Lorne Shepard and his current and former colleagues in the Learning Sciences and Human Development program within the School of Education at the University of Colorado Boulder, who inspire him and push his thinking: Kris Gutiérrez, Susan Jurow, Ben Kirshner, Kevin O'Connor, and Joe Polman.

Dan credits Michael O'Byrne, as a fellow first-year teacher, for honing his instructional design skills and setting the standard of professionalism, continued learning, and fun. He is grateful for his Interlake High School colleagues Jenny Newell, Chris Krebs, Greg Bianchi, Phil Allen, Bryce Mercer, and Jeff Ryerson. In the Bellevue School District central office, Dan thanks Nate Manning, Angie DiLoreto, Bill Palmer, Kathee Terry, and Superintendent Mike Riley, who was a remarkable educator and leader.

Dan gives special thanks to Sam Donovan, at the University of Pittsburgh, who was the first education researcher to correspond with Dan in response to a question he had as a teacher. Had Sam not answered, Dan may never have bothered to contact a researcher again. Dan is grateful for science education researchers Katherine McNeill, Christina Schwarz, Brian Reiser, Mark Windschitl, and Jessica Thompson, who have all influenced his teaching and work with teachers through their published works and personal communication. Most of all, Dan is indebted to Charles W. (Andy) Anderson, at Michigan State University. Andy's gracious mentoring, with deep expertise and patience, has carried Dan through a decade of professional growth.

We thank especially the current and past members of the Research+Practice Collaboratory, who have developed and tested a number of the strategies depicted in this book: Bronwyn Bevan, Phil Bell, Kerri Wingert, Heena Lakhani, Shelley Stromholt, Tana Peterman, Deb Morrison, Abby Rhinehart, and Andy Shouse at the University of Washington; Pam Buffington, Jo Louie, Catherine McCullough, Peter Orne, and Barbara Berns of EDC; Annie Allen, Tiffany Clark, Jennifer Ciplet, and Kristen Davidson of the University of Colorado Boulder; Jean Ryoo, Michelle Choi, Molly Shea, Meg Escudé, and Shirin Vossoughi of the Exploratorium in San Francisco; Mark St. John, Pam Tambe, and Laura Stokes of Inverness Research Associates; and Carlin Llorente, Tim Podkul, Kea Vogt, and Corinne Singleton of SRI International.

We are especially grateful to Kea Vogt, whose editorial assistance has made this manuscript more concise, accessible, and readable.

Finally, and perhaps most importantly, we give thanks to our families for supporting us in writing this book. Without the gift of their love and the time to write, this book simply could not have come into being.

This work was supported in part by grants from the National Science Foundation (award #s DUE-1238253, DRL-1626365, and IIS-1147590), the Institute of Education Sciences (award #R305C140008), the William T. Grant Foundation, and the Spencer Foundation. The opinions expressed herein are those of the authors and do not necessarily reflect those of the funders.

About the Authors

William R. Penuel is a professor of Learning Sciences and Human Development in the School of Education at the University of Colorado Boulder. His research examines conditions needed to implement rigorous, responsive, and equitable teaching practices in STEM education. With colleagues from across the country, he is developing and testing new models for supporting implementation through long-term partnerships between educators and researchers. Currently, Penuel has partnerships with large school districts and a national association of state science coordinators focused on implementing the vision of science education outlined in a *Framework for K–12 Science Education.* Penuel is currently principal investigator for the National Center for Research in Policy and Practice, which is focused on how school and district leaders use research. As a co–principal investigator of the Research+Practice Collaboratory, he has led the development of resources to help people build and sustain research-practice partnerships.

Daniel J. Gallagher is Director of Career and College Readiness at Seattle Public Schools. He previously served as the science program manager in Seattle and the Bellevue School District and taught high school biology and chemistry. Gallagher has cultivated several productive research-practice partnerships, most recently as principal investigator of two consecutive Washington State Math-Science Partnership (MSP) projects. In that partnership, multiple school districts, STEM professionals, a regional professional development provider, and science education researchers are co-developing resources to support implementation of the Next Generation Science Standards. Gallagher has also participated in research-practice partnerships spanning multiple states, in the role of co–principal investigator on National Science Foundation Discovery Research K–12 and STEM+C projects. He received his BS in biology from the University of Richmond and his master's in teaching from the University of Washington, and he is currently enrolled in the EdD program at the University of Washington, Seattle.

Index